D0848116

The Canoeist

A MEMOIR

The Canoeist

A MEMOIR

JOHN MANUEL

jefferson press

ISBN 0–97189–747–6
Library of Congress Catalog Card Number: 2006921091

In My Room
Words and Music by Brian Wilson and Gary Usher
© 1964 IRVING MUSIC, INC.
All Rights Controlled and Administered by HAL LEONARD CORPORATION
All Rights Reserved Copyright Renewed
Used by Permission

Editing by Henry Oehmig and Arlene Prunkl
Book Design by Fiona Raven

First Printing May 2006
Printed in Canada

Published by Jefferson Press
jefferson press

P.O. Box 115
Lookout Mountain, TN 37350

For my father

Acknowledgments

Many people have offered me feedback in the writing of this book, and to each of you I am deeply grateful. I would especially like to thank Henry Oehmig, editor at Jefferson Press, and A.J. Mayhew, leader of the "Tuesday morning" writing group in Hillsborough, N.C. Thanks also to my children, Jackson and Allison, for their patience and joyful presence throughout. Most of all, I would like to thank my wife, Cathy, for her unflagging support and love. She has made writing this book possible.

This book depicts actual events recalled to the best of my memory. I have changed some people's names to protect their privacy. I have made up others, such as fellow summer campers, whose actual names I couldn't remember.

All of the chapter titles, except for "Keewaydin," are named after actual rivers. My journeys down these varied waterways served as the inspiration for writing this book.

Contents

CHAPTER ONE

The Chagrin

Imagine you are canoeing in a fast-moving river. You round a bend to find yourself at the head of a dangerous rapid. A midstream boulder offers temporary refuge. You circle into the eddy behind it, still your beating heart. Perched on the edge, you scan the rapid for the best way down. An opening beckons along the far bank — a white path curving through a minefield of rocks. To get there, you must aim your canoe upstream and paddle against the current, working your way at an angle across the channel. The river rushes at you, menacing, unstoppable. You reach the open passage and turn sideways to the current. Instinct tells you to sit up straight, to keep the boat level. But the current will grab the upright paddler, suck the hull down and flip him over. Instead you must lean downstream, reaching your paddle so far as to touch the water with your outstretched hand. Do this and the river will embrace you and take you to places you have never known.

⤙

I returned to our family home on the Chagrin River in Gates Mills, Ohio, to be with my father on his deathbed. Dad had been sick with cancer for five years, living under my mother's care. The last time I'd visited, he was gaunt and irritable, but still walking and eating. I was not prepared for how badly he'd deteriorated.

Mom led the way down the darkened hall to the master bedroom. This was the room where we gathered as kids to watch television, where my parents made love, bed covers rustling on a Saturday night as I peeked in to announce my return from a date.

"Here's Johnny," Mom said.

I hesitated. Dad would want to brush down that shock of dark hair that stuck up like a cockscomb when he'd been in bed too long. The sour smell of diapers filled the room. I stepped through the doorway.

On the pillow lay a shrunken head—sallow-skinned, cheeks collapsed—and a body so thin it barely rippled the bedcovers. Death had a hard twist on my father and was pulling him down through the mattress. *Should I touch him? How can I touch him?* I walked to the bed and lifted his hand, small and frail as a child's.

"How's it goin', Dad?"

Watery gray eyes turned my way and for an instant, I anticipated his rebuke—"How's it *goin'?*"—as if I had presented him with a bottle of cheap vermouth.

But he couldn't speak. A tear welled in his eye. *Don't do this, Dad. Not now.* I let go of his hand and headed for the stuffed chair.

This was the way we did it—seated on opposite sides of the room,

eyeing each other like serpent and prey. Dad would quiz me. I would answer and wait for the inevitable put-down. About my job, my politics, my hair. I would snort, look away. It was a contest we both knew well.

But when I looked up from the chair, Dad's forearm was still raised, fingers curled. *He wants me to hold his hand. How can he want me to hold his hand?*

Mom was inspecting the forest of drug capsules on the nightstand. She could not save me. Sweat beaded on my forehead. I rose, took a step. Dad's arm fell.

Mom saw me standing. "Are you hungry? I've made us some dinner."

We retreated to the kitchen at the far end of the house, away from Dad, away from Death. Mom tied on an apron and stirred a pot of stew. I was amazed that she could care for him, cook for herself and keep up with the house. The daughter of an alcoholic father with an unpredictable temper, my mother learned to take responsibility at an early age. In our family, she was the upholder of moral order and the peacemaker between Dad and us children. She had been loyal to him through thirty-seven years of marriage and would keep him at home to the end.

I downed a spoonful of stew. "So none of the others could make it?"

Mom sighed. "Peter and Annie were here last weekend. Susie's off on some kayaking expedition in Oregon. I don't know how we'll reach her if…"

It struck me that Dad was going to die, probably within days, and that I would be the only one of his children present. Each of us kids had unresolved issues with Dad. We'd all broken his heart. Susie, the oldest, was the first to have casual sex, the first to get busted for pot. Since leaving for California in the sixties, she'd never been back for more than a week. Peter, my younger brother, was always defiant. He had bad table manners, dressed in laughably mismatched clothes, and expressed open disdain for Dad's beloved institutions — the Republican Party, Tavern Club, Yale. He actually spent his freshman year at the latter before leaving to study the sitar in India. Annie, the youngest, played the dutiful child until graduating from college, at which point she sold her IBM stock and gave the proceeds to some anarchosyndicalist cooperative in southern France.

But the tensions ran strongest between my father and me. I was the first-born son, the one he hoped would follow in his footsteps. And though I liked to think I had broken free, I was always circling back, hoping for those words of praise I was never going to hear.

Dad looked better in the morning. Daylight flooded the master bedroom through the curved picture window. Mom had propped him up on the pillow so he could see across the room. His eyes were resolute, unforgiving.

"Things are going pretty well at the magazine," I said. "I've been writing a series on canoeing."

He said nothing.

"Jackson's starting kindergarten. Allison's crawling all over the house."

Speak, Dad. Give me something. He drifted off to sleep.

Arranged on the recessed shelf above the bed were the keystones of my father's life — commendation of major from the Army Air Force, a portrait photograph from his days with the Fuller, Smith, and Ross ad agency, the gavel awarded him as mayor of Gates Mills. When I was a child, these things bestowed such power on my father. Now they seemed to mock him.

Dad woke and glanced around. "Water," he rasped.

Mom arrived as if on cue, cup and straw in hand. She sat on the bed and dipped the straw in the cup. He opened his mouth, and she dribbled the water in. "Would you like something more? How about some soup?"

Mom left for the kitchen, and we were alone again. I leaned forward in the chair. "You faded out on me."

"Happens a lot."

"What are you dreaming of when you go off like that?"

It was a bold question for me, but I wanted to know what a person thinks of when he is about to die.

"Canoeing. At Keewaydin. Right off the main dock."

What? Dad hadn't canoed in twenty years. And he hadn't been to Keewaydin since he was a boy.

"I didn't think you still cared about that," I said.

The old fire returned to his eyes. "Why wouldn't I?"

I retreated into silence. *Why wouldn't you? Because you always said I spent too much time at the river. Because you wouldn't even read the articles I wrote about canoeing. Because you never took my work seriously, not for the foundation, not for the state, not for the magazine. Because I'm the canoeist, Dad. Not you.*

Or was I? I walked down the hall into the brilliant light of the sun porch. Beyond the big picture window, the treetops swept down to the Chagrin River, dark and still in the late summer drought. This was the reason my father built this house, to gaze out on this stretch of river. I had never wondered about the name "Chagrin"; I'd always associated it with peace and beauty.

I shoved my hands in my pockets. What did my father's dream mean for him, for me? Did he wish he'd lived his life differently, followed his passion to be a creative director instead of an account exec? Spent more time canoeing? Did he really think I should work in a bank, cut my hair, and join the Tavern Club? I needed to know because he was the one who put me in that boat and set me on the river. I was doing my best to find my way, but he was standing on the bank shouting, "Johnny, come back! Johnny, come back!"

⤝⤞

The rain fell all night, and in the morning I could smell the river—rich earth borne aloft in the swirling waters. I jumped from my bed and peered into the valley. The Chagrin was near the top of its banks. Footsteps thumped up the stairs. Dad stuck his head through the door. "River's up. Want to run it?"

In an instant, I was dressed and headed down the hall. Peter lay in bed, still a few years shy of being able to canoe. But Susie was up and ready to go. We ran down the stairs and into the garage where the boats hung from the ceiling. I climbed into the attic and handed Susie the paddles and the musty Mae West life jackets. Dad backed the Country Squire out of the garage, untied the ropes from the wall cleats, and lowered the boats to the floor.

We had two boats, a Grumman canoe and a Folbot. The canoe was designed for children—fourteen feet long as opposed to the traditional seventeen feet, made of extra-lightweight aluminum with seats set close to the bow and stern. Technically, the canoe belonged to all of us kids, but I considered it mine.

Mom and Dad paddled the Folbot—a two-person kayak made of navy blue canvas stretched over a wooden frame. Dad bought it from an ad in *The New Yorker* that claimed the boat could be assembled in minutes and fit in the trunk of a car. He spent an entire weekend putting the thing together and never took it apart.

We loaded the boats on the Country Squire and headed to the put-in below the dam at Gates Mills. The dam sat at the heart of the village, its pulsating wall a magnet for people from miles around. Greaser kids came down from Mayfield Heights, their yells rising above the roar of falling water. They threw soda bottles in the river and watched them slide over the dam and spin in the backward curl of water below. My father said if you got stuck in a "hydraulic," there was no getting out. I vowed to stay away from them.

We lifted the boats off the car and eased them down the slippery path below the dam. Susie and I shared the canoe. She was a year older and got to paddle stern. I comforted myself in knowing that when she bored of canoeing, I would take that position. Mom and Dad settled into the Folbot, he in the stern. We pushed off the bank and left the manicured world of lawns and tennis courts behind.

Right away, there were rapids to negotiate—a pair of shallow ledges running diagonally across the river. The Folbot slid right over, its rubber bottom undulating over the edge. Not so with the canoe. Aluminum may be light and durable, but it sticks on rock like sandpaper. And the inch-high keel running the length of the hull made matters worse.

"Full speed ahead!" I shouted.

We made it halfway over the ledge before screeching to a halt. I pried my paddle against the bottom. "Push off," I said.

The canoe wouldn't budge.

"Rock it."

Susie scowled. "I am rocking. Stop giving me orders."

We inched our way down the ledge, each ear-splitting jerk announcing our failure to the onlookers back at the dam. Dad waited until we came abreast.

"Next time, try running that V to the left," he said. "That's your deepest water."

I glanced back to see the smooth funnel of water distinct from the abrupt drop we had come over. I could sense how the bedrock lay underneath, beveled to a flatter angle, yielding a few extra inches of water. Now I knew what to look for.

We crossed under the Old Mill Road bridge and entered the heart of Gates Mills. White-framed buildings shone through the sycamores. Henry's Tavern, where I got my Bazooka bubblegum, hugged the east bank, St. Christopher's Episcopal Church, the west. St. Christopher's was Dad's church, the spiritual gathering place of the white Anglo-Saxon Protestants who had founded Gates Mills in 1826 and still made up ninety-nine percent of its populace. Our last name, Manuel, was suspiciously Latin, but Dad, with his high forehead, gray eyes, and ever-present tweed jacket, fit the accepted mold.

Mom was Irish Catholic, pale skinned and freckled with sea-blue eyes. She raised her children as Catholics, dragging us every Sunday to St. Francis Church in Mayfield Heights, where we knelt with the Slavs, Poles, and Italians. Dad wouldn't set foot in that church, couldn't stand the sight of the black-veiled women fingering their rosaries. And yet he worshiped my mother. I sensed that despite his prejudices, he saw individuals for who they were.

We slipped past the village and entered the forest, where the dogwoods bloomed beneath the beeches and oaks. Shale cliffs rose on alternate sides of the river, waterfalls spilling through the gaps. Hemlocks clung to the steep banks, their evergreen spires reaching for the sky. These were my favorite trees. On cold winter days when snow drifted from the gray Cleveland skies, I liked to think that the deer and fox found shelter on the dry, needle-covered ground beneath the layered branches.

As we rounded a bend, a half-dozen turtles scrambled off a sandbar. These were not ordinary painted turtles that basked on every other log. The carapaces were the size of frying pans and the heads shaped like a cormorant's. I mentally scanned through my *Golden Book of Reptiles and Amphibians*, whose color drawings I'd memorized.

"Duckbills! Those were duckbilled turtles!"

Dad raised an eyebrow.

This is the wonder of canoeing rivers—every bend holds the possibility of something amazing, something new. It's not always good.

A mile down we passed the Randolphs' house perched not a hundred feet from the river. A black pipe protruded from the eroding clay bank, smelly gray liquid dripping from its mouth. Dad said this was sewage from the Randolphs' septic tank and warned us to steer away.

"Is sewage bad for the fish?" I asked.

He said it was.

"Can't anybody do something about it?"

He didn't answer. The Randolphs were his friends, just like the people who owned the steel mills in Cleveland that were killing Lake Erie and the Cuyahoga River. He wasn't going to make a fuss about it.

"River Road Bridge coming up," Dad said. "Watch out for rocks."

Just beyond the bridge, the river slid into a long rapid. We followed the Folbot down the narrow V. I love the feeling when the current starts pushing you along, like an invisible hand under the hull. Trees become a blur, the air charged with sound and smell.

"Rock," I shouted. "Go left!"

I drew hard and felt Susie pry behind. The boat angled away. We scooted past the rock with room to spare.

Mom and Dad waited at the bottom. "Slow down, Jackson. You've got a ways to go."

Jackson was the nickname Dad used for me when he was feeling relaxed. He always seemed happy out on the river. There were just not enough Saturdays when the water was high.

⇥

The front door slammed. My father's footsteps thumped across the foyer. "Where's Johnny?"

I heard Mom answer from the sun porch. "Upstairs with Peter."

At the sound of Dad coming up the stairs, I ordered Peter out. He ran down the hall, but seeing Dad's shadow on the landing, turned back and ducked into the bathroom.

Dad stood in the doorway.

"Where's Peter?"

"In the bathroom."

"What've you been doing?"

"Playing." On the floor behind me, toy soldiers were lined up for battle. His eyes dropped to my waist.

"Why is your fly down?"

At twelve years of age, I guessed my fly was down because I'd forgotten to zip it up. Dad, however, saw a darker purpose. He ordered Peter out of the bathroom.

"What were you and Johnny doing?"

"Nothing."

"Was he playing with you?"

"No!"

Peter scampered to his room, the privilege of the younger brother. Dad turned back to me.

"Were you doing what I think you were doing?"

"What?"

"Fooling around."

I could tell this had something to do with sex. He'd accused me of this before. But I had no interest in sex with boys and said so. Why did he persist in believing that? Was it because I was thin and freckled like my mother? Because I laughed too much?

"Get downstairs. You've got chores to do."

As his footsteps receded, I jumped onto my bed and cranked open the window. Dad had built a fire escape from the second-story bedrooms using pieces of pipe screwed into the siding. We weren't supposed to use it unless there was a fire, but it had become my way out of the house when I wanted to avoid a confrontation.

I scrambled to the ground, crawled past the sun porch and into the garage. The pulleys creaked as I lowered the canoe to the floor. I hoisted the boat to my knees and duckwalked it to the edge of the woods. Wrapping the frayed bow line around my hand, I dragged the canoe down the steep path, hull rattling over pebble and root. The woods glowed in the soft spring light, trillium and trout lily carpeting the ground. But I had no time to stop. I carried the boat across River Road and dropped it in the Chagrin. The hull hit with a satisfying *thunk*.

Out on the water I was my own master. One hard stroke sent the canoe surging ahead. A sweep spun it in circles. The slightest breeze could blow it off course, but down in the valley, there was rarely any wind.

I breathed in the smell of the Chagrin — growing plants, rotting leaves, wet loam — things living, dead, and in between all mixed together in the olive green waters. Downstream, the river ran deep and slow half a mile to the dam. I was not in the mood for a crowd, so I headed upstream in the direction of the footbridge.

Most people in Gates Mills live in colonial mansions with circular driveways and manicured lawns. The Cain boys lived in a dark little bungalow on the far side of the river, the only access being a rickety footbridge suspended over the Chagrin. The boys were the same ages as my brother and me, but all comparisons stopped there. The Cains were tough. If they saw me coming in my fancy canoe, they'd race onto the bridge. "Hey, kid, where'd you get that canoe? Kid, gimme a ride!"

Much as I hated their taunts, I didn't wish the Cains harm. They were part of that wild place. Like mythical trolls or a two-headed dragon, they were a gauntlet I had to pass to get to the world beyond.

Below the footbridge, the Chagrin curved away from the road between banks thick with Joe-Pye weed. I slipped around the bend (no Cain boys today) and headed for the gravel bar where the river ran free, the first rapid above the dam. A blue heron stood in the shallows, searching for minnows and crayfish. He lifted his mattock-shaped head and fixed me with a sideways stare. *Please don't fly. Let me get close.*

The heron jumped into the air, and something inside me clicked. I took aim with my paddle and fired a make-believe shot. Pow! He wheeled away and, tucking his neck into his shoulders, flew upstream on feathered oars.

I beached the canoe and stepped onto the cobbled surface of the gravel bar. The Chagrin is full of stones of all different shapes and colors, dragged down from Canada by a succession of glaciers. I picked up a piece of granite—bright pink flecked with gray—as smooth and round as a cue ball.

Against the far bank, the river cut through the gravel bar. I knelt down and peered into the depths. Something bright caught my eye—a piece of metal fluttering in the current. A dog tag. A darker shape began to appear, fur, a bright row of teeth. It was a black dog wrapped around a submerged stick. Somebody's pet fallen through the winter ice and drowned. I sagged to my knees, thinking of Carrie.

Carrie McCune was our next-door neighbor and my little sister Annie's best friend. She visited our house every day, emerging in a pink dress and hair bow from between the spruce trees that formed the border between our properties. She and Annie would set up jumps in the yard and trot around with hands held high, imaginary riders. I would sneak behind a tree and pop out as a stiff-legged monster.

"Arrrgh!"

They ran off screaming, "The ooly-ghouly man!"

Earlier that summer, Mrs. McCune called looking for Carrie. She hadn't come home from day camp, a mile's walk through the village from the Gates Mills school. I joined the search full of confidence, certain that I'd find her asleep beneath a hemlock. Like a fairy tale prince, I would awaken her with a gentle kiss and carry her back to her parents. But as the sun dropped low in the summer sky, my dream began to fade.

Searchers retraced Carrie's path from the school. At one point, she would have had to cross the millstream that ran through the elm-shaded grounds of the Chagrin Valley Hunt Club, the sanctuary and playground of the Gates Mills elite. There were two bridges over that millstream, one of which had no railing.

Mr. McCune borrowed a grappling hook from the Hunt Club Pool and began raking the muddy water. A crowd of onlookers gathered, my father among them.

Soon, the Gates Mills fire truck arrived with volunteers donning helmets and rubber boots. They urged Mr. McCune to step back. He set the hook down on the grass. The firemen stretched a rope across the millstream and two of them waded into the neck-deep water and, holding onto the rope, began walking along the bottom. They were nearing the flat footbridge when one of the firemen stopped.

"Think I've got something."

He handed off his helmet and ducked beneath the surface. I held my breath, not believing this could happen. He rose with something in his arms, a girl in a pink dress. Her arms were frozen straight up like a doll's, her face was covered with leaves.

"Get the kids out of here!"

We ran streaking in all directions as if a bomb had gone off in our midst. I sprinted across the Hunt Club lawn, heading toward home. I slowed and stopped. There was no one at home who could help me. There was no escaping the truth. I knelt before a spreading elm and put my hands on its rugged bark. *Carrie's dead. Death is real. We're all going to die.*

People streamed past me in stunned silence. I lifted my gaze. Down Epping Road, four men were walking away, heads cast down, giants in defeat. Mr. McCune was in the middle, my father at his side. Dad held his hand on Mr. McCune's shoulder.

❧

Sunlight flickered off the water. I tossed the rock in the Chagrin and headed back to the canoe. The trip downriver had passed in a dream. I carried the boat across the road and dragged it up the hill. Dad was waiting in the yard.

"Where have you been?"

"Down at the river."

"Doing what?"

"Fooling around."

Dad heard his own words. The fight went out of his eyes. He stared at the canoe, wondering, I'm certain, how this thing he'd intended to bring us together now carried us apart. But he never took the canoe away, and some years later, when I lost it in the flood-swollen Chagrin, he would buy me another.

CHAPTER TWO

Keewaydin

By mid-June, the Chagrin River is too low to paddle. Boys from Mayfield Heights wade in the shallows below the dam and throw their hooks and bobbers into the foam. They will be here all summer. The rich kids from Gates Mills are bound for "away camps" in New England, Canada, and the Rocky Mountains. At fourteen, I was sent north to Lake Temagami, Ontario, to attend Camp Keewaydin, the oldest wilderness canoe camp in North America and a Manuel family tradition.

Dad did not say it, but I knew he was sending me to Keewaydin to "toughen me up," to learn to survive away from home in a group exclusively of males. Curious to discover what I was in for, I searched the enormous bookshelf in our high-ceilinged living room for a thin volume I'd seen some years past. I ran my hands across the faded spines — novels, biographies, plays — before finding the Keewaydin yearbook. While

Dad sat in his stuffed chair reading a history of World War II, I pulled the yearbook down from the shelf and settled onto the couch.

I found his picture on page 8, posing with his cabinmates in his long-john swimsuit, hair slicked back, face stern. If any of these boys felt any sadness or fear, happiness or mischief, it was not evident in these photos. Canoe camp was a serious business.

Standing next to my father was his twin brother Bill, who died of leukemia in his twenties. Dad never mentioned Bill, other than to say he was smarter, more athletic, and more popular. I couldn't imagine what losing him must have been like.

"Is this Lake Temagami, Dad?"

"Yes. Right off the main dock."

"It's big."

"Takes a lot of paddling to get across."

The pages cracked as I turned them. "How was the fishing?"

"Pretty good. Walleye and bass. Some northern pike."

Dad didn't expand much on the past, but that left room for me to imagine. I turned the last page to find the Keewaydin logo—a bull moose framed by a triad of paddles. This was what I really wanted to see. Moose were powerful creatures, mysterious. To see a moose in the wild would mean there was still magic in the world. Had Dad seen one at Keewaydin?

"Other people saw them. I didn't."

I nodded, closed the book.

The charter bus for Keewaydin left at nine at night, timed to reach the noon ferry from Temagami the following day. Station wagons arrived in the downtown Cleveland parking lot and disgorged their cargo of adolescent boys. I gave Mom and Dad perfunctory hugs and slid my trunk into the belly of the bus.

As I stepped into the darkened interior, a couple of toughs called out, "Hey, look at this kid. Who is this dink?"

My friend Rusty sat near the back of the bus, his forehead illuminated by an overhead light. He motioned me toward the seat beside him, and I hurried down the aisle.

"Who are those guys?" I asked.

"I don't know. Must be from the West Side."

Rusty and I had been friends since early childhood. He lived across the valley, a hard bike ride up Old Mill Hill and down the County Line Road. He was the only boy in a family of three domineering sisters. Muscle-bound, defensive around my other male friends, he let down his guard with me. Together, we roamed the fields and forests along the Chagrin, hunting rabbits and fantasizing about girls.

The door hissed closed and the engine rumbled to life. Many of the boys dug cigarettes out of their packs. "Hey, Denny, throw me a Camel. None of that filtered shit." Rusty pulled out a *Playboy*.

"Have you seen Miss July? Check this out."

He held the magazine up and let the centerfold flop open. A long-legged blonde beckoned me to her bedside, turned just so to reveal the upward arc of her breasts. I shifted my legs. Something hit my sneakers — round, red, on fire.

The explosion sent my head ringing. I rocked forward, hands over my ears. The bus driver slammed on the brakes, parking the bus in the middle of Cedar Road. His menacing bulk darkened the aisle.

"Next one of you motherfuckers lights a firecracker gets thrown off the bus. I don't care if it's in goddamn Saskatchewan. D'ya hear me?"

No one, not even the tough guys, made a sound. The driver sat down. The air brakes hissed. As the bus came up to speed, we eased open the windows, leaving behind a trail of cigarette smoke, gunpowder, and exhaust.

⌀

I awoke the next morning to a different world. Gone were the rolling pastures and leafy hardwoods of home, replaced by an untamed wall of evergreens. Groggy faces stared out in silence, the hubris of the previous night spent.

Thirteen hours after leaving Cleveland, we arrived in the town of Temagami and stopped in front of the ferry terminal on the shores of the eponymous lake. We stashed our cigarettes and girlie mags under the seats (both were banned on Devil's Island) and emerged blinking in the noonday sun.

"Get your trunks and take 'em over to the ferry," the driver said. "Anything you leave is mine."

The *Aubrey Cosens* was a relic from a bygone age, a passenger ferry with the graceful lines of a turn-of-the century steamship. We hauled our trunks up the gangway, stacked them amidship, and crowded the rail. A blast of the air horn sent us cringing and whooping. The ferry rumbled out the inlet past sailboats at anchor and cabins with Canadian flags fluttering in the breeze.

As we turned onto the main stem of Lake Temagami, the shoreline receded and the cabins disappeared. A stiff wind blew out of the north.

Keewaydin, Dad's yearbook said, is an Ojibway Indian word meaning *northwest wind.* The Indians considered this a good omen, a harbinger of clear skies. But the miles of rolling whitecaps sent a chill down my spine. A boy could drown out there.

Twenty-two miles out of Temagami, the ferry slowed. Devil's Island emerged from the shadow of a low humped mountain. Green-roofed cabins peeked beneath the pines. This was it.

A tall man waited at the end of the dock, steel blue eyes beneath a high patrician forehead. In a sonorous baritone he delivered his welcome speech. "My name is Howard Chivers. You can call me 'Chief.' You're all going to have a wun'erful time…"

I snickered to Rusty. "*That's* original. The head of my day camp was called 'Chief.'"

Chief read off our cabin assignments: "Rusty Inkley, Wabueno… John Manuel, Algonquin…"

My smile faded. "Shit, we're in different cabins."

Rusty sighed. "We'll be on different trips."

The Algonquin cabin contained eight bunk beds against varnished pine logs with a pair of light bulbs hanging from the ceiling. Charlie Frasier, our resident counselor, checked my name off his clipboard and fixed me with a lopsided grin.

"Manuel. Is that like manual labor?"

"Yeah, but with an 'e' instead of an 'a.'"

Frasier pointed to an upper bunk. "This'll be yours. Right above Kittredge."

Lute Kittredge lay propped on one arm reading a science fiction paperback. He offered a barely audible "hello" and dropped his eyes back to his book. Not much promise there.

Ned Speer unpacked a pile of go-kart magazines from his trunk and set them on his bed. He straightened up to reveal a slack jaw, lanky legs and sinewy arms. I didn't normally go for jocks—Ned was a wrestler, I came to learn—but his slow, earnest smile put me at ease.

"How ya doin', John?" he said in a Southern drawl that had somehow found its way to Pittsburgh.

A boy entered the cabin dragging his trunk. Short, big lipped, with a turned-up nose and cocoa butter tan, Sandy Dalton offered a limp handshake and grinned like a chimp. "Pleased to meet you," he said in his mother's voice. Here was one kid I could pull rank on.

Chick Hancock stood exactly my height, thin and freckled like me. His smile seemed genuine, his brown eyes attentive. He and I could definitely become friends.

That would not be the case with the last of my cabinmates, the big guy in the far corner. Unsmiling, dark stubble on his chiseled jaw, he pushed a shock of dark hair off his forehead and offered me a cold greeting. "Shephard."

Along with a counselor, each cabin was assigned a guide who planned and led the trips. The guides lived in their own cabins on the far side of the island. Many were locals of French-Canadian or Indian descent.

Pete Morningstar came by the first evening, a short, round-headed man with bright eyes and a quick smile. "Manuel. Is that like manual labor?" he asked.

"Yeah, but with an 'e' instead of an 'a.'"

He squatted on the cabin floor and unrolled a topographic map. Amid the pale green rectangle were dozens of lakes—blue ovals with mysterious names like Wakimika, Obabika, and Timiskaming.

Morningstar drew a red line through the middle of a chain of lakes, forming a rough circle. "Our first trip'll last five days. We'll head up the north end of Temagami and portage into Red Squirrel. After that, Jackpine, Chambers, Ko Ko Ko. Six portages, the longest one will be about three thousand yards."

"Sir, that's over a mile and a half!"

Morningstar looked up. "That's right, Manuel. It'll put some meat on those bones."

I heard a snort and turned to face Shephard's stubbled chin, his thin lips parted in a smirk. He stared without blinking. I was going to have to shut up around him.

The next morning, we gathered in the meadow by the lodge to pack for our trip. Frasier laid out a sleeping bag, a pair of duffle bags, a box, and a canoe. "Put your clothes on top of your sleeping bag and roll 'em up together with your ground cloth. Stuff that in your dufflebag and cinch it up with a tumpline."

Frasier held up a twenty-foot-long leather strap with a headband in the middle. He wrapped it around a pair of dufflebags, tied a couple of knots to center the headband, and hoisted it onto his back.

"The bowman is responsible for carrying both his and his partner's dufflebags. The sternman carries the canoe."

Frasier moved on to the wannigan, a wooden box the size of a large cooler. Inside, cans of beef stew, peas, and evaporated milk stood four rows high and six across. "A full wannigan weighs seventy pounds," Frasier said. "Some of you scrawny boys might have trouble getting it up. Manuel?"

I stepped forward and hoisted the wannigan off the ground. Frasier had to help me get it onto my back. As the tumpline stretched across my forehead, darts of pain shot through my neck. My head wobbled like a dashboard doll. I spun sideways and dropped the box.

"You'll get used to it," Frasier said. "They do get lighter as the trip goes on."

Keewaydin used only one kind of canoe, a seventeen-foot wood and canvas, the traditional canoe of the North Woods. I stared down the length of the upright hull. Cane seats. Ribs covered with layers of shellac. Frasier said the new ones weighed eighty pounds, the older ones more than a hundred.

"Only the boys who paddle stern will carry a canoe." Frasier showed how to wrap a tumpline around the center thwart for head support and tie in a pair of paddles to act as shoulder pads. He flipped the canoe overhead, where it sat like a giant billed cap, then lowered it back to the ground.

"Who wants to try?"

Speer walked up, shaking his arms loose as if he were going into a wrestling match. He jerked the boat onto his thighs and flipped it overhead. His legs trembled from the weight of it. He threw it down and backed away.

"Gol, dang, that thing's heavy."

Shephard followed next. He got it up, puffed out his chest, and eased the boat onto the ground.

Frasier eyed the rest of us. "You don't all have to try. We only need four bowmen."

"I'll pass," Hancock said.

Kittredge shook his head. "Pass."

Dalton clucked and crossed his legs. "Surely you jest?"

All eyes looked at me. No way was I going to paddle bow. I stepped forward and closed my hands around the gunwales. The boat looked impossibly long. I jerked upward and got the hull on my knees. I lunged for the center thwart and rolled the boat overhead. Halfway up, it stopped. I staggered sideways and dropped the canoe.

That evening in the cabin, Frasier read the assignments: "Hancock, you're in the bow with Speer. Kittredge in the bow with Shephard. Dalton, you're with Morningstar. Manuel, you're with me." I turned away, tears welling. I was stuck in the bow with a damn counselor.

⌁

Dawn broke clear and blustery. We lifted the canoes off the racks and carried them down to the water. I set the duffle bags in front of the center thwart and the wannigan behind. Frasier wedged the ax behind the stern seat. I tied my rod cases—a fly rod and spinning rod—to the bow seat. Our whole world was packed into a seventeen-foot canoe.

Morningstar gave the signal and pushed off into the oncoming chop. "We've got us a Keewaydin," he called over his shoulder. "Your hat blows off, don't turn around."

I dug my paddle into the dark, clear water. The hull rose and fell, sending a clap of spray to the sides. I took another stroke and another. The shoreline passed with agonizing slowness. At this rate, it would take all day to cross Temagami. I lowered my head and paddled harder.

"You're gonna wear yourself out like that," Frasier said. "Slow your stroke down. And don't just use your arms. Lean forward, plant the paddle and bring it back with your whole upper body."

I didn't need anybody to tell me how to paddle a canoe. But I followed Frasier's advice and felt the power of my torso.

"Now, turn your blade flat as you bring it forward. It'll cut the resistance to the wind."

The canoe gathered speed. As we passed the northern tip of Devil's Island, the shoreline fell away. Whitecaps winked across the broad expanse of water. Clouds passed before the sun, changing the lake from blue to gray and back to blue again.

Our fleet settled into a loose diamond, Morningstar in the lead, Frasier and I picking up the rear. I stared at a distant point of land and watched as it slowly merged with the shore. Another point appeared, and another beyond that.

In time, I lowered my gaze. I sung to myself the Beach Boys' latest hit. *There's a place where I can go and tell my secrets to, in my room, in my room.* I fell into a trance, lulled by the creaking of the cane seats and the steady clap of waves.

"There's our portage."

Ahead the lake tapered into a cove. A faint gap in the understory of jackpine and birch marked the start of the path. We ran the canoes onto the rocks and began unloading.

"This one's about 800 yards," Morningstar said. "I'll leave my ax at the halfway mark. Bowmen, drop your wannigans there for your sternman to pick up and come back for your duffles."

One by one, the others hoisted their loads. I waited until everyone was gone, then duckwalked my wannigan over to a boulder. I squatted down, flipped the tumpline overhead and rose on trembling legs. The rocks teetered beneath my feet.

With faltering steps, I reached solid ground and started up the incline. My neck muscles fired warning shots. *You are hurting yourself. Stop what you're doing.* I pulled upward on the tumpline to ease the pressure. Step, after step, after step…

Mosquitoes rose from the mossy ground and danced before my face. I pursed my lips and blew hard. They circled behind and sank their needles into my neck.

Finally, I'd had it. I pitched the wannigan off and collapsed beside the trail. Why had my father sent me here? I was never going to make it.

At the sound of footsteps, I wiped away my tears. Hancock appeared, heading back for his duffle bags.

"You okay, Manuel?"

"Just taking a rest."

"Want some help with the wannigan?"

"I guess."

Hancock stepped behind me and lifted the box. I slipped the tumpline over my forehead.

"How far to go?"

"Not much farther. You can make it."

Dalton passed me on the way back to the put-in. He'd made it to the halfway point without stopping. I shouldn't have been so quick to judge.

Finally, the wannigans appeared, piled like Christmas presents under a small hemlock tree. When I dropped mine at the end of the row, my body seemed to rise off the ground. I walked on air back to the put-in, and shouldered the sagging duffle bags. Eight hundred yards later, I broke into the clearing.

"Get lost, Manuel?" Frasier sat in the already-loaded canoe, leaning on his paddle.

"Something like that."

Morningstar gave a nod and we pushed into a new lake.

Red Squirrel was smaller than Temagami. There were no cabins here, no boats save our own. We fanned out four abreast, our canoes skimming across the shimmering surface.

In a high clear voice, Morningstar began to sing: "Down de way where de nights are gay and de sun shines daily on de mountaintop…"

Frasier picked up the chorus, and soon we were all singing, transformed into something new, something moving as a whole.

The campsite stood on the far shore atop a sloping slab of granite. We hauled our gear up the incline and scanned the level ground.

"Put the wannigans by the fire rings and get your tents set up," Morningstar said. "Looks like the last crew left their tent poles, so you won't need to cut any new ones."

Hancock, Speer, and I claimed a rectangular patch of bare ground and unfolded the heavy canvas tent. We fastened two pairs of tent poles together with tumplines and spread them apart to make an X. Speer ran a fifth pole through the roof sleeve and hung it in the notches. We spread the canvas sides and anchored them with rocks.

Inside, the tent was dark and musty. Speer claimed one side, Hancock the other. I was happy to be in the middle, buffered from the unknown by two warm bodies. We unrolled our sleeping bags and stacked our clothes to make pillows. Speer brought out a go-kart magazine.

"You have a go-kart?" I asked.

"Heck, yeah. Six-horsepower."

"My parents said they might buy me one for Christmas," I lied. "What kind do you think I should get?"

Speer flipped through the pages and stabbed with his finger. "Turbo kart. Fucker'll go thirty miles an hour."

Hancock launched into his summer reading, *Catcher in the Rye*. "You got a go-kart, Chick?"

"Nope. A bicycle."

"Ten-speed?"

"Just a regular one."

I turned back to Speer, humbled by Hancock's honesty.

"I'm not sure my parents would get me that turbo model," I said. "Maybe the regular one."

The smell of woodsmoke drifted through the mosquito netting. We grabbed our mess kits and gathered around the fire, where Morningstar stirred a pot of stew.

"All right!" I said. "My mom makes beef stew."

Shephard mocked my enthusiasm. "All right. My mom makes beef stew."

Tears started in my eyes.

"Yeah, why don't you cry about it?"

Morningstar cut him off. Shephard must have seen me on the portage. He knew I was weak.

After dinner, I carried my mess kit to the shore and scrubbed it clean. As the leftovers sank into the depths, minnows snatched them up. I stared at the lake, its mirrored surface aglow with evening light.

Frasier lit a cigar and leaned against a log by the campfire, Morning-star beside him.

"Sir, can I take the canoe out to fish?"

Frasier frowned. "Can you handle it alone?"

"Of course. I have my own canoe at home."

"Be back by dark," Morningstar said.

I tied on the red-and-white spoon my father had recommended and cast it out to stern. "Take slow, steady strokes," Dad had taught me. "That'll create a nice wobble." I set a course parallel to shore, following the reflection of the pines.

I was glad to be alone, away from the critical eyes of the adults and the boys' constant chatter. Freed, like me, of its heavy load, the canoe skimmed across the surface. The sky darkened to violet blue. I paddled among the stars.

A cry arose somewhere across the lake, a high tremulous laugh. My heart raced with each rising note—woo *wooh*, woo *wooh*, woo *wooh*. I pictured a crazy woman, tossing back her hook-nosed face. The last note fled over the treeline and echoed across the distant lakes. *It's a loon*, I realized. *Calling out to the world, "I'm here, I'm here, I'm here."*

The rod jumped off the floor and caught on the underside of the seat. I grabbed the reel and clamped my hand over the spinning handle. The drag began to whine. Whatever this was, it was big. The fish pulled away from the boat, heading for deep water. I tightened up the drag.

For long minutes, the fish swam back and forth. Then the line stopped moving. I reeled in, felt only dead weight. Was I hung up on weeds? A dark shape emerged beside the boat—long body, head like a barracuda. A northern pike! The fish slapped the hull and charged away, pulling out another fifty feet of line. I worked him from side to side. When he drew near the second time, I slipped the net under his head and scooped him in the boat.

Frasier and Morningstar were the only ones still up by the time I made it back to camp. I carried the fish into the firelight, barely containing my grin.

"Holy shit, where'd you catch that thing?" Frasier said.

"About halfway around the lake."

"What did you catch him on?"

"Daredevil."

Morningstar took the fish by the gill. "Nice. Run about eight pounds. Gonna eat him?"

I shrugged. "Kinda stuffed."

"Clean him up, and we'll see if anyone's interested."

Word of my catch spread throughout camp. One by one, the boys emerged from their tents. As Dalton leaned in, I jerked the head upward.

"Get that thing away from me!" he shrieked.

I took the fish down to the shore and pulled out my sheath knife. Shephard appeared at my shoulder.

"Where'd you catch that thing?"

"Past that point. He took a Daredevil."

Shephard wouldn't know a Daredevil from a Hula Popper. I shoved the knife into the pike's anus and ran it up the belly. The guts pulled out easy.

❧

The dining lodge echoed with the chatter of 120 boys, each one boasting about his first trip. Waiters brought steaming plates of fried chicken and mashed potatoes and metal pitchers of purple "bug juice."

"My canoe weighs a hundred pounds," Rusty said between mouthfuls of bread. "Our guide, Buck, says it's one of the heaviest ones in camp."

Rusty was a sternman and to hear it, one of the strongest boys in his section.

"Oh, yeah? We had a three-thousand-yard portage," I countered. "Try carrying an eighty-pound wannigan over that!"

Chief rose to welcome us back and announced there would be mail in the post office. "Any care packages from home with candy and the like are to be turned over to your counselor for equal distribution."

I received two letters from Mom describing the weather at home and reminding me that she and Dad would soon be headed for vacation in France. There was nothing from Dad, but I didn't think much about it. Fathers didn't write to their sons.

❧

Our second trip ran seven days through what was known as the Obabika-Wakimika circuit. We headed north again on Lake Temagami, west across Diamond, and south into Lake Wakimika.

I'd spent two weeks at Keewaydin and had yet to see a moose. I scanned the shorelines, stalked the woods behind our campsites. Nothing.

THE CANOEIST ❧ 32

On the second morning, we entered the serpentine channel of the Wakimika River. Memories of the wildlife I'd seen along the Chagrin gave me hope. I called to Morningstar in the lead canoe.

"Sir, is there any chance we might see a moose?"

"Possible. They like to wade out and feed on the grasses. Have to be quiet, though."

I stared through the tannin-stained water to see mats of yellow grass strung out with the current along the bottom. "Hey, guys, Pete says we might see something if we're quiet."

Dalton stared, uncomprehending. He banged his paddle against the gunwale at the end of each stroke. I addressed him in a stage whisper. "Dalton!" He clucked and rolled his eyes.

Miles passed without a sighting. Each bend brought another empty sandbar, an endless wall of trees. The wilderness was not like they presented it in the picture books—a moose here, a mink there. I'd seen more wildlife in Gates Mills.

At length, the river opened onto the wide expanse of Obabika Lake. I dropped my head and settled into my stroke.

On day three we rested. After a leisurely breakfast, Frasier led a group of us across the lake to a granite bluff. The rock formation was perfect for diving, with three ledges of varying height.

I scrambled up to the first ledge, a height of maybe twelve feet. The bottom dropped away sharply, yellow-green boulders fading to blue. Diving was something I loved. You didn't have to be strong, just brave. Without hesitation, I leapt, spreading my arms as wide as they would go. The surface rushed toward me. I punched through and rose in a stream of bubbles.

KEEWAYDIN

Speer and Shephard dove behind me. Hancock jumped feet first. We climbed to the next level.

"This is as far as I go," Hancock said.

Speer frowned. "I'll jump, but I ain't diving."

I leapt out, counting the seconds in the air. The water slapped me hard on top of the head. I shook it off and swam to shore. There was one more level yet to go.

On top of his dresser, my father kept a photo of himself diving from the spar of a sailboat. He looked spectacular, arms spread, toes pointed. It was an image of Dad in a mythic past—confident, carefree—something I wanted to be. I figured that spar to be about thirty feet tall, the height of the highest ledge.

On hands and knees, Shephard and I made our way up the bluff. The view from on top was dizzying. I could see our campsite across the lake, the overturned canoes shining in the sun. Shephard turned to me. "Gonna do it, Manuel?"

He spoke without animosity, just a straightforward question.

"Yeah, I'm gonna do it."

I stepped to the edge and held out my arms. I rose on tiptoes and sprang into space. Back arched, toes pointed, I flew in perfect pose all the way down.

↔

Back at base camp, Rusty and I once again traded highlights of our trips. His canoe, it seemed, had added another ten pounds, and his portages stretched on for miles. I jacked my dive up to forty feet, but couldn't top what came next. With a dramatic flourish, Rusty reached under his bunk and handed me a small wooden canoe.

"Buck carved it for me," he said.

I turned the boat over in my hands. "Looks like *Paddle to the Sea.*"

Paddle to the Sea was my favorite book, a richly illustrated story about an Indian boy who carves a miniature canoe and paddler and sets it on a snow bank above Lake Nipigon. The snow melts and launches the canoeist on a torturous journey through the Great Lakes, the St. Lawrence River, and finally the Atlantic Ocean. Each time the canoeist is washed ashore or trapped in a logjam, someone finds him and sets him back on his journey.

I would have loved for somebody to carve me a toy canoe, but whatever it took to attract that kind of gift, I didn't have it. I had a certain wariness around men, a fear of disappointing them as I felt I disappointed my father. They sensed it and kept their distance. I handed the canoe back to Rusty.

The next trip, our last, would be a full two weeks. On the cabin floor, Morningstar unfolded his map, the edges now worn.

"We'll head across Lady Evelyn Lake and up the Lady Evelyn River. Couple of short portages gets us into the Grays River."

Drawn in red ink, our past and future trips appeared as a series of overlapping loops, each one taking us farther from base camp. This one was going way north.

"We've got a four-thousand-yard portage into Lake Makobe. It's a long one, but it will get us to the headwaters of the Makobe River. No Keewaydin group has run it in years. It's a beautiful river."

I winced at the thought of another long portage. But the chance to run a truly wild river? That was something to work for.

We left the next morning under a bright sun. A warm wind, a Wabueno, blew out of the south, pushing us along at a steady pace. *Screw the Keewaydin,* I thought. *I'll take a Wabueno any time.*

We set up camp on a barren island in the middle of Lady Evelyn Lake. Across the lake, the treeline angled gently to the peak of Maple Mountain. Earlier in the afternoon, I'd seen the horsetails streaming out from the west. Now they covered half the sky. As the sun dropped behind the mountain, the feathery clouds lit up from below.

"Look how they're changing," I breathed. "A minute ago they were pink. Now they're scarlet."

"Enjoy it while you can," Morningstar said. "It'll be raining tomorrow."

We awoke the next morning to a downpour. Water streamed off the edges of the dining fly as we huddled in our cold rubber rainsuits. The oatmeal tasted good, but it could only delay the inevitable.

We paddled all day in the rain, struggling upstream against the Lady Evelyn River. Every few miles, we had to portage around rapids. The footing was slick. My canvas sneakers were soaked. Branches drooped across the path, wiping their cold wet fingers across my face.

As soon as we made camp, Hancock, Speer, and I got out of our wet clothes and crawled into our sleeping bags. We lit candles and pulled out our summer reading. Except for Speer.

"Hey, guys, I've got a little present for you." He reached in his duffle bag and produced a small cookie tin.

Hancock looked up. "Chocolate chip! I thought Chief said we had to give those to our counselor?"

"Screw Chief," I said. "Guy needs an enema."

We devoured the cookies between bouts of laughter, scattering crumbs across our sleeping bags. No one at Keewaydin was happier than we were.

Another morning of paddling in the rain and we reached the dreaded portage into Makobe Lake. A month before, I would have had to set the fully loaded wannagin on a boulder just to get underneath it. But my shoulders had grown broad and my arms sinewy and long. I lifted the box off the ground and swung it onto my back.

The trail wound through jackpine and birch with a scattering of hemlock. It crested a ridge and angled down to a flat bog punctuated by water-filled footprints. Muskeg. A layer of live and decomposing sphagnum moss that can run several yards deep, muskeg is the curse of the Northwest canoeist. In a dry summer, it might support a man's weight, but after several days of rain, it's like quicksand.

Halfway across the bog, I came upon one of the sternmen sunk to his knees. I slogged out and called his name.

"Shep, you stuck?"

"I can't move."

"Want me to help? I'll hold the boat up."

I shed my wannigan and raised the canoe off Shephard's shoulders. He pulled his legs out of the muck and shook loose his neck and arms.

"Fucking muskeg."

"Looks like dry ground just ahead. You want to drag the boat?"

"That's okay. I can handle it."

I waited to make sure Shephard could walk, then picked up my wannigan and headed on. Step by step, yard by yard, we crossed the portage.

As we paddled into Makobe Lake, the clouds parted to reveal a fractured window of blue. The window closed as quickly as it opened, but the momentary flash gave me hope. The eye of God winking.

We aimed our canoes for a gap in the treeline—the Makobe River. Morningstar had warned us that the headwaters would be shallow. What we found was little more than a boulder-strewn path disappearing into the jackpines. The group erupted in a chorus of groans. But something about the river looked right to me. Wilderness.

We set up camp where the river left the lake. After dinner, I got out my fly rod and tied on a Gray Wulff, a passable imitation of the mosquitoes that danced around my head. I cast into the wide part of the channel and watched the fly drift with the current. The water formed a circle, and I jerked back. The fish sailed through the air and landed at my feet.

I picked it up and held it in the palm of my hand. Set in the silver sides like so many jewels were lavender bull's-eyes with the bright red centers.

"That's a native brook trout. Ever seen one of those before?" Morningstar stood on shore admiring my catch.

"It's small."

"They aren't big, but they sure are pretty. Where'd you learn to fly cast?"

"My Dad taught me. He thinks a fish isn't worth catching unless you get it on a fly."

"It's a good sport to know."

I removed the hook and put the brookie back in the stream. It disappeared in a flash, its mottled backside becoming one with the rocky bottom.

At first light, we set our canoes into the river. Morningstar led the way, prying off the bottom with his paddle. Within minutes, he was aground. We stepped out of the canoes and waded until we reached deep water, paddled another dozen yards, got out and waded.

By mid-afternoon, we'd only covered a few miles. Dalton slogged along the bottom, kicking up rocks. There was no chance of seeing anything today.

Morningstar began searching for a campsite, settling on a narrow shelf by the water's edge. As I prowled the shoreline looking for firewood, I came upon a set of cloven hoofprints pressed into the sand. They were still filling with water.

I scanned the forest for the giant ears cupped at the sound of a pursuer. I jogged forward, pushing aside branches of hemlock and alder. He was here, I was certain. Just over the next ridge.

That night I lingered by the river, cleaning my mess kit. Trees faded to black. Stars came out in the narrow band of sky. I gave up looking when I could no longer tell the water from the land.

Even in my dreams, a moose stalked the forest behind our tent. He turned his antlered head and watched me with dark, all-knowing eyes. I could still feel his presence when I woke the next morning.

"You're awfully quiet," Frasier said as we loaded the canoe.

"Hoping we might see something today," I answered.

Frasier chuckled. "You're always hoping, Manuel."

The Makobe was deep enough now that we could paddle without

running aground. A heavy mist hung over the water, jackpines rising like dark steeples. The landscape beckoned us to silence. We moved in single file, dripping paddles beading the surface with a sound like rosaries poured from hand to hand.

The sun burned the mist away, revealing banks thick with blueberries. Morningstar raised his hand.

All summer long, we'd paddled along shorelines as still as paintings. Leaves might flutter in the afternoon breeze. A kingfisher might fly from its perch. But I'd never seen anything like what we were approaching. The bushes shook as if someone, something, was trying to wrench them from the ground.

We closed the distance — twenty yards, fifteen, ten…Dalton nicked his gunwale, and the bushes exploded. The bear rose on her hind legs, a Goliath sprung from the earth. She sized us up with the eyes of a dog, raised her paws to her chest. Branches quivered as a pair of cubs hustled away, their hind ends yo-yoing into the forest. She turned back to check on her cubs, froze us with a withering huff, dropped to the ground and was gone.

❧

By week's end, Rusty and I were on the *Aubrey Cosens,* heading back to the mainland. Boys crowded the tables on the ferry's top deck, playing cards, talking loud. I recognized some of the faces from the bus ride up, but couldn't remember which ones were the tough guys.

As we turned into the northeast arm of Temagami, our ferry overtook a pod of canoes. If not for the flash of the paddles, I'd have thought the boats were standing still. For a moment, it struck me as foolish to travel like that—yard by yard across a vast, watery plain. But you didn't get tested by riding the ferry. My father knew that much.

When my friends back home asked me about Keewaydin, I would tell them about the bear, about diving from the cliffs. But the bigger stuff didn't translate into words. It was about learning to deal with kids like Shephard, about shouldering the wannigan despite the pain. It was something, too, about the slowing down of time, passing through the world at the speed of a stroke and a glide. There would be periods in my life when I would want to experience that again. But right now, I wanted to move faster.

CHAPTER THREE

The Lost

Summer of 1972: Nixon ruled the White House, the Vietnam War was dragging into its seventh year and forty-seven thousand American soldiers had come home in coffins, boys my age who'd barely had a chance to live. I had just finished four years at Yale, during which the campus seethed with discontent. Students staged anti-war protests. Black Panthers, several of whose members were on trial in New Haven for murder, roamed the streets in mirrored sunglasses and black berets, demanding we sign on to their dream of violent revolution.

Somewhere between the turgid rule of the California wing of the Republican Party and the absurd fantasies of the left-wing revolutionaries lay an answer for the country. I didn't know what that might be, but I wanted to be a part of it.

The action that summer was taking place in Washington, D.C. Presidential elections loomed in November; rallies and demonstrations filled the grassy malls. Eager, young college grads were chasing down jobs in government and think tanks. And every non-profit organization with a dream of changing the world was opening an office in D.C.

Just out of school, three friends of mine from Yale had found jobs in federal agencies. They were living together in a two-bedroom basement apartment on Capitol Hill and agreed to put me up while I looked for work. On arrival, I put my suitcase in the corner of the living room and my sleeping bag on the couch, and hit the streets in scuffed shoes and a corduroy sport coat.

I didn't want to work for the bureaucracy, fine-tuning the details of some housing program. I needed a job where I could use my writing skills to lob spitballs at the establishment. Ralph Nader was in the midst of expanding his "public interest" empire. He launched a project to publicize the voting records of every member of Congress in hopes of affecting the outcome of the fall elections. Nader needed editors to pare down his voluminous reports, and my experience as managing editor of my high school paper got me the job. I marched into the Headquarters Building in Dupont Circle, pulled up a plastic chair next to half-a-dozen other Ivy Leaguers, and started inserting periods and commas.

The honeymoon lasted six months. Nader paid us slave wages, expected us to emulate his monkish lifestyle—no car, no house, no free time. Every few weeks, without so much as a "hello," he stuck his head in our door, eyes ablaze, demanding to know the whereabouts of our director.

His self-proclaimed status as the nation's consumer advocate also started to bug me. The hotdogs I craved were poison, my father's perfectly good Corvair "unsafe at any speed." When he went after "dangerous toys," I lost all patience. If you were dumb enough to put a miniature airplane in your mouth, you deserved to bleed.

One day, Nader ordered the Congress Project staff down to the Federal Trade Commission to demonstrate for some upcoming ruling on toy safety. I was given a sign that read "Sharp Edges Make Me Cry" and instructed to walk in circles around the building. I handed in my resignation the next day.

With my job status in the air, I decided to pursue a mission I truly believed in. Environmental activism was still young in the seventies, but it struck me as something I could get behind with conviction. I scanned the Yellow Pages for "Non-Profit Organizations" and found two promising entries—the American Rivers Council and the Environmental Defense Fund, both at 801 Pennsylvania Avenue. The next afternoon, I climbed the wooden stairs, anticipating a posh suite buzzing with legions of the faithful. Instead, I found a one-room office lit by the harsh glare of fluorescent lights. Two twenty-something guys in jeans sat behind desks covered with newspaper clippings.

"I don't have any jobs right now," said the guy from the American Rivers Council. "But if you'd like to do some volunteer work—"

"No, thanks," I said. "Can you direct me to the Environmental Defense Fund?"

He pointed across the room. "That would be him."

Hard up for cash, I hired on as a sheetrocker with Grant Doe Construction Company. Grant's specialty was buying up row houses from poor blacks on Capitol Hill, renovating them, and selling them at top dollar to puffed-up congressional staffers. I followed after Hassan, the "mud man," and sanded down the plaster seams.

"Nice and light," Hassan said in a clipped Lebanese accent. "Too hard, no good. Scuff up sheetrock."

Weekdays I came home covered in white dust, my roommates in rumpled suits. But our evenings were filled with laughter and beer, and on weekends we hit the town. The beautiful Capitol Building was a short walk from our apartment, the museums and galleries just beyond. You could play pickup touch football on the Mall and hear bluegrass at the Birchmere. The city was full of smart, young people riding the crest of a change. The future, we were certain, was ours.

So I was stunned when Nixon got re-elected. His deceit, his meanness was so obvious to me. Now he was back on the throne. But no sooner was Nixon inaugurated than the walls began to crumble. Congress mounted an investigation of the Watergate break-in, and Nixon's henchmen began to talk. Calls rang out for Tricky Dick to resign, none louder than the largely Democratic denizens of D.C.

One afternoon, someone organized a "Honk If You Think He's Guilty" rally in front of the White House. I raced over from work in my dirt-covered Mercury Capri and drove in circles on Pennsylvania Avenue, horn blaring, long hair streaming out the window. This was a great city!

With so much attention on politics, I all but forgot about rivers. The Potomac was always visible, just beyond the monuments, but its broad, muddy expanse didn't hold much appeal. Then my roommate, Edward, urged me to check out the Great Falls of the Potomac fifteen miles upstream.

On a crisp fall afternoon, he and I walked out on the bluff on the Maryland side of the river. Ed had told me the falls were spectacular, but nothing prepared me for this. The bedrock shuddered from the force of falling water. A fine mist rose with the updraft. The Potomac narrowed to a stone's throw in width and thundered over a series of ledges seventy feet tall. The falls looked fatal if run in a canoe, but downstream, the river flowed through a navigable gorge. All I needed was a canoe.

Mid-December, I drove back to Gates Mills to celebrate Christmas. Mom had the house looking beautiful as always — Christmas tree in the sun porch, stockings above the big stone fireplace, white pine branches circling the staircase. I was glad to see her and Dad, my sisters, Annie and Susie, and my brother, Peter. Susie was writing for a newspaper in Nevada after a stint as a rafting guide. Peter was back from UC Berkeley, where he was majoring in ethnomusicology. He'd studied the sitar in India and was dressed in what looked like white pajamas.

Dad invited both Peter and me to the annual Christmas party at the Tavern Club. This was a fraternity for Cleveland's WASP elite, housed in a Tudor mansion in a formerly grand neighborhood, now a black ghetto known as the Hough. Peter, the budding Marxist, refused to take part in this "bourgeois charade." But at Mom's insistence, I consented, putting on a coat and tie and slicking back my shoulder-length hair.

Dad was full of good cheer at the club, announcing to his friends that I was "just out of Yale." I smiled and shook hands, got buzzed on champagne. But on the ride home, he began to snipe about my job.

"I sent you to college so you could sand sheetrock?"

"Don't worry, Dad. It's not forever."

It must have confused him that I would put on a coat and tie for the holidays, enjoy drinks with his friends, yet refuse to consider a career in business.

"Stuey Harrison said he might have something down at Cleveland Cliffs. Why don't you give him a call?"

"Yeah, right. They're the ones dumping crap into Lake Erie!"

Dad scoffed. "You and Nader. You think you have all the answers."

The next morning, I avoided Dad at the breakfast table. I walked into the sunroom and stared at the Chagrin. The river lay fringed in ice, the sky hung leaden gray. This was no time to go canoeing. But come spring, the water would be up in D.C.

Dad had bought the Grumman for all of his kids to share, but I was the only one who cared about canoeing anymore. The boat was just sitting in the garage, so I asked Dad if I could take it with me to Washington. He stared at the newspaper, took a bite of his English muffin.

"Fine. I'm taking it," I said.

⚓

On the first warm weekend in April, I drove out to Great Falls with the canoe strapped on Styrofoam mounts to the roof of the Capri. The parking lot across from the Old Angler's Inn was crowded with cars, many with roof racks designed for boats. I undid the cross strap I'd run through the open window and lifted the boat overhead. Its familiar weight felt good on my shoulders.

I followed the Billy Goat Trail down to the river. People stood on the rocks at the big bend of the Potomac, watching a group of kayakers surf the rapids. I was jealous of this new breed of paddler. They could bob through the waves without taking water and roll upright after a spill. But I figured with a little practice, I could do almost anything in my canoe that they could.

My plan was to put in at the top of the bend, make a quick run through the rapids, then turn around and try some of that surfing. Easing my boat into the water, I felt a twinge of fear. The current looked powerful, stronger than anything else I'd ever paddled. But I could see only one serious obstacle—a large rock in the middle of the bend.

The instant I left shore, the current grabbed the hull and swept me toward midstream. I was moving so fast that I couldn't gauge which side of the rock to shoot for. Too late, I chose the inside passage. The boat clanged against the rock and threatened to capsize. I grabbed the gunwales, and rocked it back to level, half-full of water.

The kayakers watched stone-faced as I paddled through the next rapid. I angled toward shore, trying to act nonchalant. One of the kayakers broke free of the group and peeled in beside me.

"You all right, buddy?"

"Yeah, I'm fine."

"I can't believe you're out here with no life preserver. That's exactly how people drown."

"I was just running that one rapid."

"One is all it takes," he said.

He eyed the water-filled hull. "You ought to get some floatation for that thing."

"Floatation?"

"A Styrofoam block, inner tube, something to keep your boat on top of the water if you swamp. We've already had four drownings out here, and the Park Service has threatened to close the river if we have any more."

Screw you, asshole. You and your dick-nosed kayak. He was right, of course. This antique canoe was a joke. I was a joke. I couldn't run a simple rapid without hitting a rock. Avoiding the stares of the bystanders, I dumped out the canoe on the bank and hauled it back to the car.

❧

The phone rang late one night. My roommate, Flint, came bleary-eyed from his bedroom before I could answer it. He handed me the receiver.

"Hey, Johnny boy, I hear you're hanging out with a bunch of your Yale buddies. How about letting me stay with you for a few weeks while I look for work?"

Stephen Furman. I knew he wouldn't be away for long. Stephen was one of my best friends from high school, a jokester with a reckless streak that both enticed and scared me. Stephen brought wonder and mischief to my life, but it always seemed to come at a price.

I had been a straight-A student before Stephen enrolled at University School, prone to making wisecracks under my breath, but never doing anything that would compromise my grades. Within months of his arrival, I was in the back of the classroom, purposefully falling over in my chair to show off for my newfound friend. My grades plummeted.

It wasn't that Stephen had no interest in learning. He paid rapt attention to the teachers he admired but skewered the ones he found tired and boring. Sleepy Phil, a doddering teacher of American history, liked to lace his lectures with long-winded anecdotes about the derivation of modern idioms— "three sheets to the wind," "break a leg." Stephen would wait for him to finish, then pronounce loud enough for the back row to hear, "Ah, ya lyin' bag of shit!"

I was glad to have Stephen as a friend, but I wasn't sure how he would fit in with my D.C. housemates, serious politicos who believed in working within the system.

"We don't have much room down here," I said. "I'm not sure Ed, Ken, and Flint want anyone else in the apartment."

"Just tell 'em I've got some dynamite weed."

With the understanding that Stephen would only stay as long as it took him to find work, my housemates allowed him to come. Stephen unrolled his sleeping bag on the other couch next to mine. Soon we were both sanding sheetrock by day and laying awake at night listening to the Grateful Dead and talking of Stephen's newfound fascination with Eastern mysticism.

As I predicted, Stephen's stay lasted months, not weeks. He couldn't find the job he wanted with the American Friends Service Committee. My housemates tolerated the cramped living conditions, but they were bewildered when Stephen insisted upon shifting their political discussions to a spiritual level.

"You guys gotta understand. Nixon can't escape his own karma. Babba Ram Dass says— "

"What the fuck are you talking about?" Flint rolled his eyes.

One weekend, Ed and Ken invited their girlfriends down, which meant we had seven people staying in the apartment. Someone flushed the wrong thing down the toilet, and the water backed up and spilled out of the bowl. We were sitting on the living room floor playing cards when this foul-smelling liquid began to ooze onto the carpet. We climbed atop the couches while the water continued flowing from under the bathroom door. Tampons and toilet paper floated among the playing cards. Ken called the landlord, who arrived shortly afterward and stared in disbelief at the people and the wreckage. He pointed a finger at his two unsigned tenants and their guests. "All of you, out!"

Stephen and I were glad to be on our own. We found a one-bedroom apartment beneath the shady elms on East Capitol Street. We bought a used couch and a pair of double mattresses. We made grocery lists, and I complied with Stephen's request for soybeans and tofu. I even helped him hang his poster of the Buddhist Wheel of Life in the living room.

Then, after a few weeks, we started to clash. We disagreed over who spent how much money for what. We argued about how long Stephen was gone with my car and when he'd promised to be back. Some days, we could hardly stand the sight of each other. Other days, we got along like old times.

Stephen took a job as an elevator boy at the Rayburn Building, the 5:00 PM to midnight shift, so I didn't see much of him during the week. We both missed each other. One night, he invited me to meet him after work. We sat out on the Capitol steps and while the guards strolled around the corner, lit up a joint and stared out at the city.

"You ought to run for office, John. You've got the looks. You make friends easily."

"Nah. Could you see me putting on a suit and asking people like my father for money? 'Hey, man, I *really* need your support! Asshole!'"

Stephen laughed. "Your dad's not a bad guy. He's got more integrity than most men I know. He's always polite, always talks to me whenever I come to your house."

"Yeah, I suppose. He paid my way through college."

"And summer camp. And that trip to Africa."

I felt nervous when Stephen talked like that. It was so much easier when I could make fun of Dad and not acknowledge the love he had for me and my siblings. Love carried a mutual burden of responsibility. I wanted to be free of it from time to time to do what I wished.

Weekends we slept late, made waffles, and read *The Washington Post*. In the afternoons, we liked to drive out to the parks in Maryland and Virginia—Mount Vernon, Great Falls, Harpers Ferry. Sometimes I would take the canoe, but without another car to leave at a take-out, I couldn't paddle far.

One day, I read an article in *The Post* about a place called the Lost River. "Listen to this, Stephen. 'The Lost River meanders through the West Virginia countryside before disappearing into the side of a mountain. It emerges several miles downstream—'"

"Hey, I've got a buddy who lives in Lost River. We need to check that out."

On a Friday afternoon in April, we loaded the canoe on the Capri and headed across the Appalachian Mountains to West Virginia. Stephen's friend Ludwak was waiting for us, joint in hand, on the front porch of the spruce-shaded bungalow he shared with his senile father.

Ludwak looked like a Rubens satyr, flaming red hair and pointed goatee. He talked loud and fast, seemed friendly enough, but there was a bitter edge to his voice, something dark inside.

He invited us in and told us to put our sleeping bags on the leather couches in the living room. The Ludwak family home was crafted with handsome woodwork and furnished with beautiful antiques. Stephen told me that Ludwak's father had been a judge; clearly he was a man of taste.

A radio blared from one of the bedrooms. Ludwak stuck his head through the door. "Turn that goddamn thing down! I've got company." Then wheeling around, he said, "Old man's nuttier than a shithouse rat."

I couldn't believe someone would talk like that to his father. When Ludwak left the room, I asked Stephen what had happened between them. He didn't know.

After dinner, Ludwak set us to work rolling joints. He had a pro-digious supply of marijuana, which he claimed to have planted and harvested along the West Virginia roadsides. "These people are so stupid they can't tell cannabis from Joe Pye weed," he said. "I come right behind the road crews when they mow the shoulder and pick the stalks up."

By 10 PM, I was too wasted to speak. Stephen and Ludwak guf-fawed into the night, smoking joint after joint, reliving their college pranks. This wasn't my style, getting high all the time. Stephen's reck-less streak had been entertaining in high school, but it was wearing thin. I was tiring, too, of his love affair with Eastern spirituality—the belief that you couldn't alter your destiny. It seemed like a cop-out to me, a reason not to think for yourself. I retreated to the living room and curled up on the couch.

Saturday morning, we followed Ludwak in his pickup truck to the take-out on the Lost. The river lay out of sight on the far side of the valley just beneath the brow of a wooded ridge. The highway wound downhill. Ludwak pulled onto the shoulder and motioned for me to park.

"Take-out's down this path. Leave your car here and put your canoe in the pickup."

I peered through the leafless trees. "Have you ever seen where the river goes into the mountain?"

Ludwak sniffed. "Heard about it, never seen it. For all I know, the guys who named this river were high on something. They probably paddled upstream by mistake, and when the river petered out, they made up some bullshit about it disappearing into a mountain. Fuckin' hillbillies."

We stopped laughing when we reached the put-in. The Lost was so shallow it looked to be paved in cobblestones. I asked about putting in farther downstream, but Ludwak knew of no other access.

"Hell, it's only five miles to the take-out," he said. "Worst comes to worst, you can walk the damn thing."

Stephen and I bid Ludwak farewell. We turned and faced the river.

"You take the stern," Stephen said. "You're the one who knows how to paddle."

"Want me to call out the rocks?"

"Fine."

Stephen crammed himself into the bow, his knees rising high over

the gunwales. It had been some years since I'd paddled this canoe tandem and I'd forgotten how small it was.

We pushed off the bank and paddled to midstream, prying off the
bottom all the way. Fifty yards along, we ran hard aground.

"Backwater," I said.

We pushed our paddles against the bottom. The boat wouldn't
move. I commanded Stephen to rock backward, the tactic I'd used on
the Chagrin to dislodge the canoe from the shallow ledges. Still, the
boat remained stuck.

"You need to get out," I said.

Stephen stepped into the ankle-deep water and lifted the bow off
the rock. We paddled another ten yards and ran aground.

"Backpaddle," I said. "Jerk it."

Again, I ordered Stephen to dislodge the canoe. He slumped in his
seat. "Why do *I* need to get out?"

"Because the bow is on a rock, that's why."

Stephen yanked the boat sideways. We struggled on. Rocks littered
the channel, preventing us from paddling in a straight line for more
than a few yards.

"Draw left. Left!"

The canoe screeched to a halt. Stephen slammed his paddle down.
"Will you quit yelling?"

"I'm not yelling."

"You're ruining the whole fucking mood."

"Fine. I'll *speak* the orders instead of shouting them."

I composed myself as best I could. "Go left," I said, as we approached
the next minefield of rocks. "Now, right. Right!"

We banged against the rock and yawed to one side.

"This is *not* going to work, Stephen."

"All right," he said, "Try this. I'll point which way we should go, and you turn the boat in that direction."

"What?"

"I point. You turn."

I shook my head. "Every time you point, you'll have to let go of your paddle."

"Let's. Just. Try it."

The current picked up speed, the rocks came on fast. Stephen pointed to the left, took two strokes, pointed to the right. We hit and swung halfway around, coming aground sideways to the current.

"This is bullshit," I said.

"All right, let's just try paddling without talking."

"You mean *feel* our way through? This is not a Zen archery course, Stephen. This is a fucking river. I know how to get down these things."

I couldn't believe this was happening. We'd had such high hopes for this day — the wild boys cruising down a river, hawks circling overhead. Maybe this hole in the mountain would make up for it.

We pried the boat loose and paddled on. As the river grew deeper, I stole glances at the wooded hillside. The trees were just budding out. In another week, everything would be in bloom.

We came upon a grassy cove at the head of a narrow gorge. An old log cabin — the remains of one — stood in the middle of a wheat-colored meadow. We pulled ashore and circled the ruin. The log walls had collapsed. Through a warped window frame, I glimpsed rusted mattress springs and tattered newspaper. Someone had planted daffodils around the foundation, and I thought of the hopes they must have had for their little home. What had happened to cause them to leave?

"You wanna eat?" Stephen asked.

"Yeah, sure."

"I'll get the cooler."

We sat on a log and ate our sandwiches in silence. Stephen announced he was going for a walk. I lay back amid the daffodils and closed my eyes. The light came and went as clouds passed before the sun. I stretched my arm across my face, rolled onto my side. Thunder rumbled close by, and I looked up to see an enormous black cloud welling over the ridge. Stephen came running across the meadow.

"Man the boats!"

We launched into the river, hoping to outrun the storm. I heard a sound like gravel being poured from a dump truck and turned to see the river's smooth surface transformed. The raindrops hit with the force of BBs. We hunched our shoulders and fled into the gorge — no choice now but to paddle on.

Lightning flashed and thunder exploded in shock waves between the walls. With our knees hugging the wet aluminum hull, we were the perfect lightning rod.

And yet we were zooming untouched down the rapids. We slid down chutes and bounced through tail waves.

"Hey, Stephen, we're doing good!"

"Yeah, too bad we gotta die!"

Hemmed in by the canyon walls, the river ran deep, the current swift. For once, Stephen and I were working as a team. We were actually having fun.

All too soon, the river widened and the current slowed. The rain subsided. Thunder faded into the distance. I glanced at the hillside and caught the reflection of sunlight on glass.

"There's the car," I said. "We must be getting close."

I rose up on my knees and scanned the river ahead. Would there be a dark hole like the mouth of a cave? A gigantic whirlpool? The ridgeline turned, the river narrowed. Yes, the water did disappear among the rocks, but the cleft in the ridge left no secret as to where it led. This was nothing more than a boulder-clogged channel, the remains of some ancient rockslide.

Stephen frowned. "This is it?"

"Guess so."

"I thought the guy said it disappeared into the side of a mountain."

"That's what he said."

"Ah, the lyin' bag of shit."

We circled once around the muddy pool and hauled the canoe out onto the bank. Stephen sat down and rolled a joint. I turned the canoe over. Dozens of new scratches marred the hull. One of the aluminum ribs had popped loose.

"This doesn't look too good," I said.

"Ah, fuck it."

Stephen passed the joint. I took a long hit, grew dizzy but not high. Canoeing reveals the truth about relationships. Two people bound together, same goal, different responsibilities. How you react when things get tough says a lot about your ability to live together. Overall, Stephen and I had not performed well.

I passed the joint. "Remember Mr. Nelson?"

"Bud Nelson? Lives in Cleveland?"

"Yeah. He's a friend of my Dad's. He's started something called the Ohio Conservation Foundation. He wants me to work for him."

Stephen exhaled. "What, he just called you out of the blue?"

"No. I was talking to him when I was home over Christmas. I told him about that bill to create a Cuyahoga National Recreation Area. I said I could help promote it."

"Back in Cleveland?"

"I could start out here. But he said eventually I'd need to go back home."

There, I'd said it. A slow fire burned in my chest. The last of the clouds were clearing the ridge.

Stephen lay back in the grass, his eyes gone liquid.

"You'd be good at it," he said.

CHAPTER FOUR

The Cuyahoga

The Manuel men have a long history with the Cuyahoga, the river that gave rise to the founding, and for more than a century, the prospering of the City of Cleveland. The *John S. Manuel,* a steamship named after my grandfather, wound its way up the Cuyahoga from Lake Erie for forty years, delivering iron ore to the steel mills built along the banks. My uncle David owned a small tanker, the *Marine Fuel Oil,* that plied the same stretch of river, refueling the ore carriers before their return trip to the mines in Minnesota and Upper Michigan. My father's office on the twenty-second floor of the Illuminating Co. Building looked down on the mouth of the Cuyahoga, its dirty brown tongue protruding into the ashen gray of Lake Erie.

The summer after my junior year in high school, I worked as first mate on the *Marine Fuel Oil,* scraping and painting the deck and manning the lines when we went out to fuel an ore boat. Its berth was a rusting bulkhead five miles upriver from the lake in an area known as the Flats. This was the heart of Cleveland's industry—a serpentine floodplain covered with railyards, refineries, and steel mills. Day and night, smoke billowed from the big stacks of the mills and blue flames from the thinner stacks of the refineries. The sky shimmered hazy white, the air reeked of petrochemicals and asphalt.

Most of the time I worked alone, pushing a three-inch-wide paint scraper across the hot steel deck. Fifty yards away on the other side of the river, hammer mills banged inside the windowless expanse of the Republic Steel Mill. A fine, red dust rained down from the smokestacks, coating the deck, my car, my back.

At least once a day, a deep blast from an air horn startled me from my work. I turned to see a tugboat straining around the bend, ropes tethered to the bow of a giant ore boat. The siren sounded on the Jefferson Street Bridge, and the trestle rose until one end pointed straight up in the air. Yard by yard, the ore boat came into view, tall as a grain silo, longer than a football field.

If the ship needed refueling, Stan and Eddie, co-captains of the *Marine Fuel Oil*, drove down from their homes on Cleveland's West Side. I put away the paint scraper and cast off the heavy, oiled ropes, as Stan fired up the twin diesels and steered us upriver to where the ore boat was docked.

I loved cruising the Cuyahoga on the *Marine Fuel Oil*, the black steel prow parting the oily brown water. I leaned against the rail in jeans and a T-shirt, nodding at the mill workers who came out to eat lunch at the river's edge. Office towers commanded the high ground, but I didn't envy the lawyers and accountants stuck behind their desks. I was a river man, a working man.

The Cuyahoga was a lifeline to the steel mills, but you didn't want to fall in it. The water was a witch's brew of municipal sewage, effluent from the mills, and spilled oil from boats and tank farms. Biologists said the lower Cuyahoga was devoid of life, caustic enough to peel the paint from a ship's hull. I remembered seeing piles of oil-soaked debris float past the tanker one day and, driven by an onshore wind, drift back upstream the next.

Two years after my stint as first mate, the Cuyahoga caught fire. A spark from a welder's torch drifted down from a bridge and ignited the oil-soaked surface. At first, no one thought to call the fire department. Oil patches had ignited on the river before to no great effect. But this fire spread to the shipyards of the Great Lakes Towing Company. Black smoke filled the air. Fire boats converged on the scene.

I was out of the country when the incident occurred, but I laughed when my parents showed me the infamous photo in the *Cleveland Plain Dealer* of a fire boat aiming its water gun at the burning river. The Cuyahoga was already dead. This was just its cremation. Lake Erie was dying, too, its shoreline littered with rotting fish, its beaches perennially closed. No one in the position to do so had the will to stop the pollution.

But then things began to change. The fire on the Cuyahoga became the rallying point for a national environmental movement. Articles decrying the pollution of our water and air appeared in newspapers and magazines. Citizens marched before legislatures. Congress passed the Clean Water Act, calling for the nation's rivers to be "swimmable and fishable" by 1983. Across the country, non-profit organizations sprung up to push this new environmental agenda. One of these was the Ohio Conservation Foundation.

❧

Annie sat at the dining room table reading the latest revelations about the Watergate scandal in the newspaper. "I can't believe you voted for Nixon, Dad. He's such a crook."

My father put down the sports section, glanced at my younger sister, then rested his eyes on me. "I suppose I should have voted for McGovern. Then we could nationalize the steel industry."

"Darling, don't exaggerate," Mom said. "You know he didn't propose that."

Peter sat next to me in his Indian *kurta* pajamas. He made a spitting sound, poked through his half-chewed eggs, and raised his forefinger aloft. "Out, out, damn shell."

Mom buried her face in her hands. Her children were hopeless when it came to table manners.

Dad shook the paper. "When do you start work, Johnny?"

"Monday."

"How about your apartment?"

"I'm moving in tomorrow."

"I suppose you could ride the rapid transit with me."

"No, Dad. We're on different lines."

Dad stood up, brushed the crumbs off his corduroy pants. Mom rose with him. "Well, come back on Friday," she said. "You and Dad can hit some tennis balls."

The Ohio Conservation Foundation occupied a three-room suite in a once-fashionable arcade in downtown Cleveland, now housing a tired collection of wig shops and beauty parlors. Cleveland had slid downhill since its heyday in the 1950s, when it was the eighth-largest city in the nation. Many corporations had moved their offices out to the suburbs or left town altogether. Even the steel mills were closing down, rendered uncompetitive by the more efficient Japanese.

But I was part of the new paradigm, Cleveland as the gateway to a reborn Lake Erie with parks along the Cuyahoga, clean water and clear skies. Each morning, I put on a coat and tie and rode the rapid transit to work. I emerged from beneath the Terminal Tower, strode across Public Square and up Euclid Avenue.

Tony, the foundation's executive director, greeted me with a jovial smile. A former college basketball star turned king of the Cleveland slow-pitch softball league, Tony was nominally committed to saving the environment but preferred glad-handing Chamber of Commerce types to confrontational politics. That suited me fine; we needed the androids' support to advance our agenda. And it allowed me to focus on my strength—writing.

"Hey, Shakespeare," Tony said, "I've got to give a speech to the Rotary Club. Write me some of that purple prose. But leave out the stuff about saving that woodpecker."

"The pileated?"

"Yeah, that one. I always say it wrong."

My chief mission was to build support for a Cuyahoga Valley National Recreation Area, the bill for which was awaiting action by Congress. Though the Cuyahoga was a wasteland in its lower reaches, twenty miles upstream the river flowed through a rustic valley dotted with historic farms and bisected by hemlock-shaded ravines. The Ohio and Erie Canal, built in the early 1800s to connect Lake Erie and the

Ohio River, paralleled the Cuyahoga, its locks and towpath still in serviceable shape. Our plan was to turn that towpath into a bike trail and use the nearby train tracks for a scenic railroad.

In the mid-1970s, America was mired in a fuel crisis spawned by an Arab oil embargo. Gasoline was in short supply, and prices were high. The federal government supported a policy of developing recreation areas near major population centers. Northeastern Ohio was home to five million people with few places to go besides the municipal parks. And right in their midst lay twenty thousand acres of undeveloped land.

Selling the "burning river" as worthy of a national recreation area designation wasn't easy. The Cuyahoga would never be declared a Wild and Scenic River. But I made a point of distinguishing the valley from the river, the middle Cuyahoga from the lower. In magazine articles, speeches, and slide shows, I waxed eloquent about the white-tailed deer and the red-tailed hawks, the historic Hale Farm and stunning shale staircase of Brandywine Falls.

Throughout the project, I maintained hope for the river. The Cuyahoga was as pretty as the Chagrin in places and sported some decent rapids near Akron. But one problem was that Akron's sewage treatment plant emptied into the river just upstream from the proposed park. The plant processed both waste water from homes and businesses and storm water that ran off city streets and parking lots. In dry weather the plant could handle both loads, but after heavy rains, it was overwhelmed. Raw sewage flooded straight into the river and could leave the water toxic for weeks thereafter.

I asked water quality experts if there were times when the river would be safe to canoe.

"Probably," I was told. "But you never know what the weather's going to do, so it's best to tell people to stay off it."

"Can't they upgrade the plant? The river could be a real asset to the park."

"Someday, kid. Someday."

Away from the job, my life veered between loneliness and an all-too-comfortable routine with high school friends and family. Weekdays, I returned to my downtown apartment, made dinner for one, and worked on a novel about two boys playing outrageous pranks on a town much like Gates Mills. I went home on the weekends, slept in my old bedroom, and ate dinner with my parents before going out with friends.

While Mom fixed dinner in the kitchen, Dad and I sipped martinis in the sun porch. He asked about work as usual, and I described my latest brochure.

Dad nodded vaguely. "Stuey Harrison's got a position in the accounting department."

"Jesus Christ, Dad, I've *got* a job."

It started to dawn on me that I could not live and work in the same town as my father. When spring came, Tony closed the office early on Fridays. He had softball practice at five, and I got into a pickup game of the same sport with some friends in Hunting Valley. I was crossing Public Square headed for the rapid transit when I saw Dad coming the other way. I tried to blend in with the crowd, but he searched me out and blocked my path.

"Where do you think you're going?" he said.

"Home."

"Home? It's 4:30."

"Dad, it's Friday."

While a crowd of office workers streamed past, my father lectured me on the value of working an eight-hour day. He swiped his hand across my long hair and jabbed at my gaudy necktie. The old rage welled inside of me. He would never be happy until I conformed to his image of a man. That meant putting on a gray flannel suit to work for some dying industry, joining a country club full of old white men, and burying the dream of a creative life.

Monday morning I walked into the office to find Tony at my door wearing an impish smile. "You're in luck, Shakespeare. Sierra Club is sponsoring a canoe trip down the Cuyahoga. They want somebody from the foundation to join them. I think I've got a game that weekend."

He handed me the invitation and headed to his office. "But you can bring me back some of that granola stuff."

The morning of the trip, I packed my camera gear and an extra set of clothes and headed south on Interstate 271. This might be the perfect opportunity to take some photos for a brochure. The clouds were breaking up after an all-night rain, the soft air redolent with the promise of spring.

The interstate crossed over the Cuyahoga valley, treetops colored pastel green and pink. I took the next exit and followed the two-lane road down to the valley floor. A trio of cars with canoe racks sat parked beside the Ira Road bridge. I pulled in behind.

"Hey, you must be the guy from the foundation." A tall, red-headed man approached with outstretched hand. "I'm Ron Kovacs, president of the Sierra Club chapter."

"Nice to meet you."

Two heavy-set boys wearing thick wool jackets paced before their canoe. "That's J.P. and Larry. They're both new members." And experienced canoeists, no doubt. Larry looked especially convincing in his Australian digger hat.

"Over here we've got Vic and Dennis..."

The pair waved quickly and returned to packing their boat.

"Grab your gear and we'll be ready to go."

Beyond the grassy knoll, the Cuyahoga streamed like a giant conveyor belt, cocoa brown, aswirl with rips and boils. I sniffed the air — sewage. The banks were draped with what looked like wet toilet paper.

"What's that on the bushes?" I asked.

Ron sighed. "We got a good drenching last night. That darned Akron treatment plant must've overflowed."

I walked to the bank, felt a chill rising off the water. "Must be in the fifties. You sure we should be running this?"

"Heck, yes, it's gonna be a beautiful day!"

Ron read out the boat assignments: "J.P. and Larry, you're in the yellow canoe. Vic and Dennis in the red. John, do you mind paddling bow with me?"

Oh, great. The bow. Usually, I didn't mind paddling up front, but when you don't know the stern paddler, the bow can be unnerving; you can't see what he's doing, and it's hard to correct for mistakes.

"Fellas, John and I are going to be running sweep. I've got a whistle, so if anybody gets in trouble, I'll give three quick blasts. That means stop immediately."

I knelt down in the front seat. The boat wobbled as Ron stepped in the stern. I made sure my waterproof camera bag was sealed and strapped to the thwart. Clothes I could afford to lose, but not my Canon.

"Let's paddle out and wait for the others," Ron said.

We pushed off the bank and paddled to midstream. I drew on the left to get the bow headed into the current. As the stern fishtailed behind, Ron let out a frantic yelp. I turned to see that he'd fallen backward on the seat, feet in the air. He pulled himself up, face gone white.

Now I was scared. Capsize in this filth, and you were bound to get sick. I glanced at the bank. Still time to back out.

Vic and Dennis flashed by in their yellow canoe. J.P. and Larry followed, gripping their paddles by the shafts. Ron yelled after them, "Hold your paddles by the handles. By the handles!"

We turned and followed, swept along in the fast-moving current. I squatted down on my haunches. This canoe wasn't going anywhere but straight ahead.

As far as I could see, every branch along the bank was snagged with human refuse — toilet paper, tampons, condoms. I called over my shoulder. "Hey, Ron, we should declare this a Wild and Septic River."

"What?"

Around every other bend, a tree lay fallen in the river. "Strainers" are a canoeist's worst nightmare, often suspended right in the path of the main current. Water will flow around a rock, but it goes under and through the branches of a tree. If you hit a strainer in a canoe, you'll be turned sideways and flipped. You could be washed downstream, or you might get snagged.

Dennis shouted a warning as each strainer came into sight. Ron and

I charged for the opposite bank, but J.P. and Larry were slow to react, clearing the outstretched branches by the slimmest of margins.

"How far to Peninsula?" I asked.

"Should be coming up shortly."

Peninsula is an historic riverside town that park supporters billed as a guaranteed attraction. This was where people would come to rent bikes and shop for antiques. A scenic railroad running up the valley would stop here. Maybe someday an outfitter would rent canoes…

A low bridge appeared, marking the approach into town. I caught a glimpse of Victorian rooflines, the train-station-turned-café. We could be in there now having coffee.

The buildings soon fell behind, and the river widened. The interstate towered over the valley on giant cement pillars. From up there, I'd once glimpsed a hemlock-shaded ledge just upstream on the Cuyahoga. This could make a cover shot for a brochure on the park. It might be the only such ledge on the whole damn river, but I wasn't above selective imaging.

I took my camera out of the dry bag and screwed on a telephoto lens. The hemlocks came into view, but the ledge was gone, submerged beneath the swirling plane of the flood-swollen river. My plans for air-brushing the Cuyahoga were as hopeless as my dreams of creating a life in Cleveland independent of my father. What the hell could I do?

Beyond the interstate, the Cuyahoga meanders through a broad floodplain. Riverview Road parallels the floodplain; the passing drivers look out over cornfields and forests. But from the seat of a canoe, all I could see were head-high banks of clay. I felt as if I were paddling through a drainage ditch.

"Strainer!" yelled Ron.

The tree appeared at the inside of the bend, a red maple toppled by a recent flood. Vic and Dennis drew hard to one side, missing the topmost branch by inches. J.P. and Larry never had a chance. They hit the tree sideways and capsized. Both paddlers disappeared.

Ron blew his whistle: "Boat over!"

We flew past the tree as the canoe rolled to the surface. J.P. clung to the stern. Larry popped up downstream, his digger hat strapped to his chin.

Ron shouted to Vic, "Grab the canoe. We'll get Larry."

The current swept Larry to the outside of the bend and along the sheer mud wall. He clawed at the bank like a cockroach in a toilet bowl. Each time he gained a handhold, the dirt gave way, and he slipped helplessly beneath the surface.

I spotted some bushes hanging just above the river. "Let's stop him over there," I yelled.

We angled toward shore, pinning Larry against the bank. Ron grabbed a branch and the canoe jerked to a halt. I hoisted myself on the bank and prepared to grab Larry. Behind me, the bushes crackled to life. A furry brown shape dove into the narrow gap between the canoe and the bank. Two more followed, each disappearing into the water before I could tell what they were. A fourth hit the gunwale and tumbled at Ron's feet. A baby beaver.

Ron pulled his knees to his chest. "Get him out!"

I let go of Larry and reached for the beaver. He clicked his front teeth. I jerked my hand away.

"Get the beaver out!"

I reached for the hard, stubby tail and lifted the animal in the air. "Who'd ever think something like this could live in the Cuyahoga?" I said.

"Get rid of it," demanded Ron. "And help Larry, for Christ's sake."

I'd forgotten about Larry, clinging to the gunwales. I tossed the beaver into the river and grabbed Larry by the collar.

"Can you make it up?" I asked.

Larry shook his head. I mustered all my strength, leaned back and hauled him onto the bank.

"How ya' doin', man? You gonna make it?"

Larry rose to his knees, water dribbling out the upturned side of his hat. His eyes were unfocused, his complexion bone white. His lips began to quiver as if he might speak. Instead, he leaned over and barfed in the grass.

CHAPTER FIVE

The Upper Haw

The interstate ran south from Cleveland to Bluefield, West Virginia, terminating at the blue-green wall of the Appalachians. A two-lane highway began at the end of town and switchbacked up the mountain. At each turn, the horizon fell farther below. I crested the ridge and entered a new world of mountain laurel and galax.

The road hugged the contours of the land, dipping and rising through tawny meadows and stands of white pine. Holstein cows stood watch on the hillsides. Down in the valleys, sunlight glinted off rushing water.

I nudged the Capri toward the guardrail, hoping for a better view. The streams danced just out of sight, revealing themselves in flashes between sycamore and maple. At each crossing, I recited the names on the little green signs — Big Reed Island Creek, Clear Creek, Laurel Fork. I would come back for them someday.

Just past the town of Max Meadows, the road ran onto a long steel-truss bridge. The New River emerged from between low green hills, breathtaking in size, tumbling over pure white ledges. All across the surface, the current rippled and twirled.

More lights flashed upstream. I slowed to a halt. These beams were bold, somehow winking longer and larger than the water. I struggled to see through the glare. Paddles!

The canoeists were still a hundred yards off when the horn of a pickup sent me on my way. I crossed the river and headed up the ridge-line. The asphalt ribbon wound through Hillsville and Fancy Gap. Mountains marched across the horizon. I shifted into fifth gear, felt myself flying. This was the Promised Land.

Just past the North Carolina state line, the highway began to drop. Switchbacks that had lifted me up only hours before pulled me down into the hazy piedmont. I watched the mountains disappear in the rearview mirror, felt the heat rise off the land. I closed the window and turned on the air conditioning. By the time I reached Chapel Hill, I was thoroughly depressed.

The road coming into town wound up a wooded hill lined with Victorian homes and low stone walls. Franklin Street leveled out beneath an archway of elms. Students appeared on the sidewalks wearing flip-flops and cut-off jeans, and beyond them stood the Colonial brick buildings of the University of North Carolina.

I spotted a girl ahead of me, riding a ten-speed against the flow of traffic. Her long white legs slowly worked the pedals. Blonde curls tumbled over broad shoulders. She glanced over but didn't notice me, her wide cheekbones tapering to a half-smile. "I'm gonna meet that one," I said to myself.

I drove to the end of Franklin Street and into the town of Carrboro. The apartment stood on a treeless lot before a string of high tension lines. I parked next to a beat-up Ford Pinto and hauled my suitcases inside. The manager came out of his office and led me to the room across the hall. He jangled his key in the lock and flicked on the overhead light. Linoleum tile floor, wicker furniture, plywood cabinets…what a piece of shit.

I put my clothes in the bureau and the clock by the bed. Shoes went in the closet, toiletries in the pink-tiled bathroom. My face in the mirror looked utterly forlorn. Blue eyes drooped, bearded cheeks sagged. I lay down on the bed, overwhelmed by this cheap, soulless home, and began to cry. What was I doing here? Why had I left everyone and every place I'd known?

I fought to remind myself why I'd come — to earn a master's degree in environmental planning, to start a new life away from my parents, to find a new river, to find love.

Classes were still a week away. I wandered the streets, sat on the stone wall in front of campus and watched the faces go by. The woman with the blonde curls was nowhere to be seen.

Following the sounds of laughter in the night, I walked into an open-air bar. The courtyard was packed with students, all of whom seemed to know each other. They spoke a language I didn't understand.

"Carver's here with Missy."

"Ah naay!"

"I got me a new truck."

"Ass grite!"

I finished my beer and drifted out to the sidewalk. Walking back to my apartment, I came upon a narrow building with a promising sign: Haw River Paddle Shop. I peered through the window at a dark shape suspended in air—a canoe.

The door stood open the following morning. The proprietor nodded as I stepped inside, brown eyes watching through an orb of curly black hair and beard. I glanced at the knives in the display case, the paddles on the wall. The canoe hung from the ceiling, forest green, just like the ones at Keewaydin. I ran my fingers along the hull.

"That's ABS," the man said. "Brand new material. Vinyl on the outside and foam in the middle. Slides over rocks like you won't believe."

I walked around the bow. "How much does it weigh?"

"About seventy pounds. More than aluminum, but a lot less than wood and canvas."

The man came out from behind the counter. "You aren't from around here, are you?"

"Nope. Ohio."

"Is your name John Manuel?"

I turned and stared.

"I'm Jim East. I was in your brother's class in high school."

It took me a minute to recognize the face inside the hair. "East! My God! What are you doing here?"

"Came down to be near my dad. He split up with my mom. He's living over in Durham."

I laughed. "I came here to get *away* from my dad."

We talked of our siblings, Peter's latest trip to India, Susie's job as a rafting guide in California.

"Are there any rivers down here?" I asked him. "I didn't see anything after I left the mountains."

"There's a nice one south of town called the Haw."

"Any rapids?"

"Hell, yes. The Upper Haw's mostly Class Is and IIs. The Lower's got IIs and IIIs. It's shallow right now, but it'll come up in the spring."

I confessed that I wasn't familiar with this new river terminology.

"Class I is basically a riffle or a little ledge like that one below the dam at Gates Mills — anything you can run straight on. Class II rapids require some maneuvering — a series of standing waves or an S-turn around some rocks."

Jim's eyes grew wide. "Class IIIs are like big drops with a keeper hole or a twisty passage in the middle. If you get off line, you're likely to dump or pin your boat."

I felt a twinge of nervousness. "Do they go higher?"

"Oh, yeah. The ratings run up to Class V, but you don't want to be messing with that."

I examined the price tag on the boat. "$850! Guess I'll be renting."

Jim shrugged. "I've got lots of rentals. But you really ought to have your own boat. I've got some factory seconds coming in next month. They came out of the mold with soft noses, but you can patch 'em up with a fiberglass kit."

He paused for a moment, patted the nose of the canoe. "I'll sell you one for five hundred dollars."

My own boat. A full-sized boat. I could run a river anytime, anywhere, without worrying about reserving a rental or getting back before the shop closed. I could outfit the boat the way I wanted, raise or lower the seats. And I could invite other people. That girl with the blonde curls.

It would be a major responsibility. I'd have to find a place to store it. I'd need to fiberglass the bow and refinish the wood gunwales every year. I'd worry about scraping it up on the rocks, or worse, losing it altogether. Was I ready for that kind of investment?

My boat arrived at the shop in mid-September—a 16-foot Mad River Explorer, fire-engine red with blonde wood gunwales and cane seats. I bought some two-by-fours and gutter mounts to make a roof rack and drove the canoe back to my apartment.

Several days passed before I could muster the courage to patch the nose. The materials were new to me—fiberglass cloth and epoxy glue in two parts, a clear resin and a hardener. Once you mixed them together, there was no delaying or turning back.

I laid the cloth against the bow and brushed on the epoxy. Jim said it was important to put down enough layers to protect the bow from hard knocks but not so much that it wouldn't cut through the water.

As I smoothed the strips along the hull, I thought of all the people who, through the ages, had labored over canoes not so different from this one. Four thousand years ago, this was a dugout canoe hewn from the bole of a cypress or red cedar. Later came the birch bark canoes, their lightweight skins stitched by Native American women to bent ribs of cedar or spruce. In the nineteenth century, French-Canadian and English fur trappers introduced the wood and canvas canoe, the likes of which I'd paddled at Keewaydin. The development of aluminum aircraft in World War II led to the manufacture of boats using that lightweight metal. And now we had evolved to hulls made of thermoplastics. All of these embraced the same basic design — a narrow hull curved upward at both ends, durable, transportable, the essence of simplicity.

I let the epoxy dry overnight and put on a second layer. When this dried, I sanded the edges until they merged smoothly with the hull. I drove the boat down to University Lake and set it in the water. The trim looked good from front to back. The cane seat crackled as I eased myself down. I took a few forward strokes and let it glide. Nice and straight. I had myself a boat.

Then came fall. The campus oaks glowed like burnished copper, and the humidity vanished into the deepening blue sky. The sun shone day after day, something that never happened in Cleveland. I made new friends and fell under the spell of life in Chapel Hill.

Over Christmas break, I went back to Cleveland. I looked forward to returning to our house on the hill and the friends I'd known since childhood. Despite his differences with me, Dad was always welcoming. I was comforted to know that he and Mom would always be there, always be together. Someday I would find a woman to love as much as my father loved my mother.

Dad was mollified that I was back in school, though he was baffled as to why I had chosen the South. We sat in the sun porch, the winter light dimming over the ice-covered Chagrin.

"So, are you actually planning to settle down there?" he said.

"Yeah, why not?"

"Big fish in a small pond."

"You know, Dad, there are actually some smart people in North Carolina. They come to UNC from all over the country."

I shook my head. Surely, Dad knew that I could no longer live in the same town as he. He didn't approve of my career path, rarely showed any warmth. Why would he be bothered if I settled somewhere else?

I didn't stop to wonder what it must have been like for my parents to have all their children move away from home. Susie was now a journalist in Hawaii. Peter had moved to Los Angeles. Annie was in college in Connecticut, me in North Carolina.

Mom came in with trays full of sherry and soup. She asked how my grades were. I told her they were fine.

"Will you be coming home this summer?" she asked.

"I don't know, Mom. We'll see."

In January, I vacated my apartment and moved with two friends into a board-and-batten-sided bungalow off of Franklin Street. The house wasn't much to look at, but the hardwood floors felt good underfoot, and the big double-hung windows in the front bedrooms let in the morning sun. I bought a queen-sized mattress, which covered half the bedroom floor. The sudden expanse made it all the more clear — I needed a woman to share this with.

A classmate invited me to a party at her house in the country. She told me the house was in the middle of a cow pasture and had been abandoned for twenty years before she and two other women decided to rent it.

"We heat with wood and get our water from a well," she said. "You'll like it."

Old Highway 86 ran north from Chapel Hill through moonlit pastures and leafless stands of sweetgum. I turned into the rutted driveway, drove a quarter mile through the dark and parked next to a line of mud-spattered pickups and Volvos.

The farmhouse stood beneath a pair of giant oaks, windows aglow like a ship at sea. I parked and strode toward the front porch. Something caught on my leg, and I splayed out onto the ground. What kind of idiot would string a barbed wire fence around her house?

I knocked, and as the door opened, I stared in astonishment at the woman with the blonde curls. She introduced herself as Cathy.

"Sorry about the fence," she said, seeing the tear in my pants. "We put it up to keep the cows away from the daffodils."

Wide cheekbones, green eyes, thin lips slightly parted — she was as pretty as I remembered.

"I think I saw you riding a bike on Franklin Street once," I said.

She looked surprised. "When was that?"

"Back in August. Just before classes started."

A shy smile crossed her face. "You have a good memory."

Cathy led me into a room crowded by men with beards and pony-tails and women in jeans and hiking boots. My friend, Pat, was making hash brownies in the kitchen. I struck up a conversation with her, keeping an eye on Cathy.

"You weren't kidding when you said this was out in the country," I said.

Pat laughed. "I see you found the fence."

We talked of the rickety house and the bemused farmer who rented it to "three purty women" for free in return for their putting out the occasional bail of hay for the cows.

I slipped back through the crowd to find Cathy alone in the corner.

"So, what is it you do?" I said.

"Instructional design."

"You mean like how to use magic markers to draw on a poster?"

"That could be part of it."

She launched into an explanation of her job at the university, of which I didn't hear a word. I stared at her eyes, the alluring gap in her front teeth. Other guys tried to interrupt, but she politely dismissed them.

I left that night with an offer to come back and help her cut firewood. This gave me the opportunity to show off my prowess with a chainsaw and to discover that her love of the country, her sense of independence, was real. She had also come to North Carolina on her own, leaving her home in central Florida to break away from her parents and the conservative politics and mores of her home town.

A few days later, she asked if she could come in to use my shower before going to work. The third time she visited, I waited in the bedroom.

"Why don't you leave those off?" I said, as she emerged with her change of clothes.

We blackened the pavement over the next few months, driving the twenty miles back and forth between town and country. It would have been easier to move in together, but we were cautious people. She wasn't sure if I was interested in a long-term relationship. I wasn't sure how she'd handle a canoe.

Come the first of May, I popped the question.

"Sure," she said. "I'd love to go canoeing. But I've never done white-water."

"I'll teach you."

Jim agreed the upper Haw was the best place to take a novice paddler. I'd paddled it several times and thought it's mix of flatwater and easy rapids would be a great introduction for Cathy.

We met at the canoe shop on a Saturday morning and followed Jim's battered pickup truck into Chatham County. I still wasn't enamored of this piedmont landscape, the mangy patchwork of second-growth forest and tobacco fields, the red clay banks like open wounds along the road-side. To me, it felt claustrophobic. But the rivers were another matter.

As we clattered out onto the wooden bridge, I beamed like a proud father. "There it is."

The Haw stretched dark and lovely between the arching boughs of sycamores. You could trace its path all the way to the horizon, clouds floating above the gray rocks. This was a room with a view.

We parked beside the bridge and carried the boats down to the water. I had outfitted my canoe with kneepads, a Styrofoam block for floatation, and bailers front and aft.

"Clip your dry bag to the thwart," I said. "Just in case we go over."

I held the gunwale while Cathy settled in the bow. "How's it feel up there?"

"Good."

We pushed off and followed Jim out to midstream. Cathy had a good stroke. She gripped the paddle with one hand atop the handle and the other at the bottom of the shaft. Her movements were strong, but unhurried.

"Try leaning forward when you place the paddle; then draw yourself upright," I said. "That way, you use your back muscles instead of your arms."

Cathy had a great-looking back—broad shoulders tapering to a narrow waist. I worried that her pale, freckled arms would sunburn easily. But she'd grown up in central Florida and spent the last five years in North Carolina. She knew how to take care of herself.

The current picked up speed, spidery boils rising from the depths. "Those are nothing to worry about," I said. "But if you see a stationary V like that one, there's a stick or a rock right beneath the surface. Stay away from those."

Cathy nodded. I liked that she didn't feel the need to talk. She scanned the banks with a serene smile, followed a crow as it flew across the channel.

Jim called over his shoulder. "Sawtooth Ledge coming up. Stay to the left."

"Okay, John, tell me what to do," Cathy said.

I asked her to show me a draw stroke. She pivoted to the right, planted her paddle in the water, and drew the blade toward the hull.

"That's good. Now, reach way out."

She took three powerful strokes, pulling the bow across the water.

"Perfect. That's all you'll need for now."

Jim went first, hugging the inside of the bend, riding the deep water along the bank. We ducked beneath the overhanging sycamores.

"Keep us against the bank," I told her.

A broken line of white roostertails marked where the ledge angled in from river right.

"Get ready with that draw," I said. "When we come to the ledge, look for a V facing upstream. That'll be the deepest water."

Jim darted into midstream to avoid a cluster of rocks. Cathy leaned out and dug her paddle in deep. We popped into the sunlight and bore down on the ledge. I took a few quick strokes to straighten out the stern. We slid right down the V.

Jim waited in an eddy at the bottom of the rapid, watching us with furrowed brow. As we flew past, Cathy swatted the water with her paddle and sprayed him in the face.

"Hey, you!" he sputtered. I laughed as if I were in on the plan, but this girl took us both by surprise.

Below Sawtooth, the river slowed. I settled into the rhythm of camp days, long strokes and steady breathing. I scanned the banks for wildlife. The forest grew to the river's edge, river birch and elm, hackberry and oak. Among the deadfalls on the bank, I found what I was looking for.

The snake lay stretched on a log. It was at least a yard long, heavy bodied in the shape of water snakes. The dark crossbands and bullet-like head, I recalled from my old reptile identification book, were trademarks of the Northern water snake. I brought us in close.

Cathy leaned away. "I don't like snakes, John."

"It's not poisonous," I said.

"I don't care. We had water moccasins in Florida. They weren't something you fooled with."

I moved Cathy away. The snake was on the verge of molting, its eyes covered by a milky sheen. I waved my hand in front of its face. Its yellow tongue flicked the air.

"Does it see us?" Cathy asked.

"It knows something's near. It can feel the heat."

"Why doesn't he move?"

"It's half-blind, for one."

Cathy frowned. She may have appreciated the knowledge, but she was never going to warm to snakes.

We paddled around the bend to where the Haw rippled through a scattering of rocks, what river runners call a boulder garden. Jim suggested a lunch break.

We picked out a flat rock in midstream and beached the canoes. I laid down my life jacket as a seat cushion and stretched out my legs. The rock felt warm against my calves. I tilted my face to the sun.

"Beer?" Jim asked.

I hesitated. Didn't we need to be on our toes?

"Relax, man," he said. "This is the upper Haw."

Cathy took out her Swiss Army knife and cut up an apple. She did the same with a hunk of cheese, then placed the slices in my mouth. No one had ever done that for me.

At intervals across the channel, the current parted around the big gray rocks. The Haw had sculpted them into graceful curves, Henry Moore reclining nudes. One held a neat pile of tiny clam shells in its belly.

"What do you think left those?" I asked.

"Probably an otter," Jim said. "Haw's full of 'em."

I studied the tall stand of loblolly pines on the far shore. A white spot stood out against the dark green of the needles. Suddenly, it sprouted wings and soared out across the river.

"That's a bald eagle!"

Growing up, I had learned that bald eagles were destined for extinction. Like Lake Erie and the Cuyahoga River, they were victims of an unavoidable byproduct of commerce—pollution. The eagle might be America's national bird, but you didn't sacrifice agriculture or industry. Finally facing the eagle's imminent destruction, Congress passed a law banning the use of DDT. This was the pesticide farmers sprayed on their fields, that then ran into the rivers, was swallowed by fishing-eating birds and fatally thinned their egg shells. Here was proof that the law was working.

The eagle swooped down and raked the surface with outstretched talons. "He got one!" I cried.

As the eagle flew downstream with fish in tow, I threw my hands atop my head and danced in circles. Cathy beamed. Jim looked amused. The sighting more than made my day.

With the sun straight overhead, we packed up the canoes and headed back on the Haw. Jim paddled out front, eyes on the river ahead. Cathy took half-a-dozen strokes, laid her paddle across the gunwales, and took off her life jacket. She crossed her arms and lifted her T-shirt over her head. She wasn't wearing a bra.

The sight of her breasts, just the outermost curve, caused me to stir in my seat. What would it be like to make love to her in this canoe? She could lie behind the center thwart....

Cathy refastened her life jacket and picked up her paddle. "I'm ready," she said.

Just ahead the river narrowed, the rush of falling water suddenly growing louder. The current picked up speed. Jim's canoe dropped over the edge.

"Here we go," I said.

The rapids came into view, blinding in the sunlight. I leaned into my stroke, drove the canoe toward the open V. White tongues lapped at the hull. The shoreline blurred.

"Keep paddling. Faster!"

The rapids came one after another—Beginner's Peril, Little Nantahala, Final Solution. We moved in perfect harmony, switching sides, whooping, delirious. We rode the last tail wave, exhausted but wanting more. The current slowed, the river widened.

For a time, we didn't speak. We paddled among the islands where the air hung thick with the smell of honeysuckle.

"Did you like it?" I asked.

"Yeah, I liked it."

The Bynum dam appeared on the horizon. We angled toward the bank and beached the canoe next to Jim's.

"You guys did great," he said. "I'd say you're ready for the Lower Haw."

Cathy and I exchanged proud grins. I grabbed the stern loop and waited for her to lift the bow. She watched Jim disappear down the trail, then came back and parted my lips with her tongue.

CHAPTER SIX

The Lower Haw

Below the dam at Bynum, the Haw River begins its descent toward the coastal plain in earnest. Gone is the pastoral river that wanders between clay banks. The Lower Haw pushes among the rocks and islands, intent on reaching its juncture with the Deep River and then to the ocean.

Boaters who take on the Lower Haw must possess the basic skills of whitewater paddling. Tandem canoeists must be able to read the river, to communicate and react with assuredness and power. They must know their draw strokes, their pries and reverses. And if the river is running high, they must be able to seek shelter in the eddies behind the rocks, to bail a waterlogged canoe and scout the river ahead.

On a Saturday morning in spring, I stepped onto the front porch of the log cabin Cathy and I had rented and peered through the tall grove of loblolly pines. The sky was clearing after an all-night rain. The Haw would be up. The question was how high?

Cathy poured a bowl of food for Sydney, our black lab and surrogate child. Syd was a tough dog who'd grown up on Cathy's farm and fought for his place among half-a-dozen mongrels. One of our requirements in finding a place to live was having some woods nearby where Syd could roam. The house also needed to be within commuting distance of my job at the State Energy Office in Raleigh and Cathy's job at the university in Chapel Hill. By sheer luck, we happened upon this rental house in Durham at the end of a one-way street. It even had a shed where we could store the canoe.

I went back inside and dialed the Haw River Paddle Shop. "What's the river at?" I asked Jim.

"A foot and a half."

"Whoa!"

"You guys can handle it," he assured me. "We're meeting below the dam at eleven."

I covered the receiver. "It's a foot and a half."

Cathy frowned. "That's higher than we've ever done it before."

"We'll be all right."

"Okay," she nodded.

I loved this about Cathy—her physical bravery, her trust in me as a paddler. In the two years we'd been canoeing together, we'd become a good team. We'd graduated from the Upper to the Lower Haw, run the Nantahala and the Chattooga.

The decision to move in together had been scary for both of us. I had turned down an offer to return to Cleveland to be assistant director of the Ohio Conservation Foundation. Cathy had moved away from her friends at the farm. We found we were becoming good companions, not given to vocalizing our fears, but comfortable with each other in an unspoken away. Step by step, we were growing as one.

After living together for a year and a half, we decided to get married. We didn't ask one another, just agreed it might be the next thing to do. We announced our intention to family and friends. Two months later, we called it off. The prospect of committing to something permanent was too scary for both of us. I could not see the end of that river, could not know what rapids lay ahead or what skills I might need to run them. We decided just living together was good enough.

⊸⊷

Jim stood in the gravel parking lot by the Bynum Dam fastening a spray skirt to his waist. Like many other canoeists in recent years, he had switched to paddling a kayak. I felt betrayed by his conversion. Canoeists formed a community bound by a love of the craft, its tradition, beauty, and versatility. But I understood why he'd made the change. Kayaks were more maneuverable and watertight than canoes. And if you paddled solo, as virtually all whitewater kayakers do, you didn't have to worry about a partner screwing up.

I had considered buying a pair of kayaks with the thought that Cathy and I might both learn to paddle them and venture out on more challenging rivers. But she'd never expressed an interest in kayaking, and I knew that if I made the switch, we would stop running rivers together. Sticking with tandem canoeing meant that I might never paddle the big water—the Ocoee, the Gauley, Section IV of the Chattooga. But that was a sacrifice I was willing to make.

Two of Jim's friends were already in their kayaks, paddling in place against the runout from the dam. I'd never seen so much water coming over the top. The air reverberated with an ominous chugging, a gargantuan steam engine buried in the river.

"Watch yourself today," Jim shouted. "River's got a lot of push."

Cathy and I tightened the straps that held our thighs snug against the hull. This was one of several features I'd added to enhance our comfort and performance, along with foam kneepads and air bags for floatation in the bow, stern, and midsection.

We paddled along the base of the dam to get clear of the near shore rocks. Then we turned and followed the kayakers through the twisting rapids.

Jim glanced at the hand-painted gauge on one of the pylons of the Bynum Bridge. "One foot five inches. River's dropped but not by much."

The current slowed for a brief stretch and the noise of the dam faded. We drifted beside the Bynum Mill, its brick walls shrouded in kudzu vines. Mills like this one dotted the banks of rivers throughout the piedmont. Jim said that most were built in the late nineteenth century before the widespread availability of electricity. The natural gradient of the rivers, concentrated in one spot by the construction of a dam and millrace, provided the power to run the machinery.

On the hillside above the mill, small woodframe houses peaked through the oaks. Mill owners like Luther Bynum had built these houses for their workers to lure them off their farms. He added a company store, a school, a Baptist church and a Methodist church—everything a person needed to survive. But there was no room for dissenters in this paternalistic environment, only for loyal workers.

The mills boomed through the 1960s, then one by one they fell silent, run out of business by cheap foreign labor. Ex-hippies from Chapel Hill were buying up the houses in Bynum, moving next door to the families of the former mill workers. Theirs was an uneasy truce that occasionally flared out in public, arguments over what to do with the abandoned mill and the aging Bynum Bridge. Compromises were made; life went on. The river never stops.

We fanned out four abreast, paddling into the morning sun. We chatted about the Red Clay Ramblers' latest bluegrass performance, the new Chinese restaurant on the edge of town.

Ahead, the Haw braided among a phalanx of wooded islands, with channels of varying width and depth. Despite having run the Lower Haw several times, Cathy and I were still unsure of the best way through this maze. New channels were open at the higher water level, many of which we'd never explored.

"Which way, Jim?" I asked.

"Middle right should be open."

Jim led the way into a pale green tunnel, sunlight filtering through budding ironwood, river birch, and oak. Warblers called back and forth, cerulean flashes in the understory. We glided fast and silent, the lapping water masking the sound of our approach.

A flash of movement caught my eye—something big sprinting through the underbrush. Wings fanned out. A wild turkey! It flew out over the channel, so close Jim could have touched it with his paddle. The turkey soared into the woods, angled left and right and was gone.

Jim shook his woolly head. "River magic," he said.

We emerged from the woods into a clamorous, sunlit stretch. Whitewater surged around a broken ledge.

"Head right!" I called.

Cathy drew on one side; I swept on the other. We rode the curving tongue past the twin boulders and drank in the rapid's fading applause.

Gathered at the base of the rapid, we exclaimed about our near misses and great moves.

"Did you see me clip that rock?"

"That was totally awesome!"

Cathy and I bailed the water out of the canoe, while the kayakers relaxed.

We passed beneath the Highway 64 bridge where the Haw begins a steady drop. The treeline recedes. The river sweeps through a boulder-strewn landscape. Running down the middle is a long series of standing waves dubbed Ocean Boulevard. Today, it looked especially menacing.

Cathy and I slid into the first set of waves, alternately paddling and freezing as the bow rode up the crests. Water splashed over the gunwales and filled the space between the air bags. By the time we'd cleared the second set of waves, the water was over my knees.

"Eddy out," I hollered. "We need to bail."

We angled for a boulder on river left with a small pool behind. As we crossed the eddy line, the boat slowed its forward motion — "stalled out" in river lexicon — while the stern swung in a violent arc. My heart leapt as the canoe yawed halfway over and rocked back to level.

While Jim and his friends waited downstream, I unclipped the plastic milk jug and started to bail. Eight, nine, ten scoops of water — it took forever to drain the boat. I took the sponge from under the air bag and sopped up the muddy remains.

"Okay, babe. Let's go."

To get out of an eddy and into a fast-moving current, you need to paddle upstream, otherwise you'll be pushed back against the shore. Once the canoe is out of the eddy, you must turn sideways and lean downstream, letting the current push the nose around. Your instinct is to lean upstream to counter the onrushing current, but instincts are not always right. The current pulls down on the upstream side of the hull and will capsize the canoe if you're not careful. The way to stay afloat is to lean downstream, bracing yourself against the water with the flattened blade of your paddle.

But I was not yet a believer. I held myself erect going into the turn. Then, as if a giant hand had reached under the hull, the boat began to roll upstream. I grabbed the gunwale, leaned away. But we'd passed the tipping point. I took a frantic breath as we tumbled into muddy darkness.

The Haw held me under for just a matter of seconds, but when I broke the surface, Cathy was yards ahead. Her hair was sprung out like Medusa's, her arms backpaddling to slow her descent. Voices called for us to get away from the boat. I rolled onto my back in the defensive position, arms out and feet up. A boulder loomed ahead. I swam for the eddy behind and dug my fingers into its jagged face. Cathy crawled onto a rock downstream. At least we were out of the river.

As we huddled on our separate islands, the canoe drifted away. It was approaching the head of another rapid when Jim raced out and drove it ashore with the nose of his kayak. The boat now, too, was saved. But how to reach it?

I let go of my rock and swam down to Cathy's. We found that we could touch bottom and stumbled downstream to where Jim waited with the swamped canoe.

"I guess they mean it when they say you have to commit to the lean," I said after I'd caught my breath.

Jim nodded. "Thought you guys would've learned that by now."

Cathy and I exchanged sheepish grins. We rolled the boat upside down and, straining against the vacuum of trapped air, lifted the stern and drained out the water.

I held the gunwales while Cathy climbed aboard.

"You okay?" I asked.

"Yeah, I'm okay."

"Ready to go?"

Cathy nodded. Once again, we had to paddle out of an eddy into fast water. This time we both leaned downstream. I was afraid of tilting that boat, putting the hull on edge. But I could feel it reach equilibrium with the current. The boat swung around and leveled out.

We didn't have long to relax. Gabriel's Bend, the Haw's most challenging rapid, lay around the next turn. Gabriel's Bend lies in perpetual shadow, tucked in a narrow channel between an island and a steep hillside. The gradient drops sharply at the head of the channel, kicking up waves that can run for fifty yards. When the Haw reaches a foot and a half, the waves are so tall and steep they form troughs or "holes," notorious for stalling or swamping a canoe.

This time the rapids were big enough to warrant scouting, so we beached our boats on the bank and followed Jim through the twisted trunks of mountain laurel. The trail ended at the head of the rapid. Jim had to yell to be heard above the roar.

"There are a couple of holes in this first set of waves and another over there on the left!"

I played out the possible routes in my head. If we stayed to the right, we might swamp in the first set of waves, to the left we'd run into the second. A nimble boater might be able to weave a path between them, but Cathy and I were unlikely to do that in our sixteen-foot canoe.

"Should we just run it straight?" I asked.

Jim pointed. "Don't forget the pillowed rock."

At the bottom of the rapid lay a boat-sized rock half-submerged in the middle of the channel. Water poured over the flat surface then curled back on itself—a "keeper." This kind of rapid could trap a boat if you went into it sideways.

I caught Cathy staring hollow-eyed, and put my hand on her shoulder. "You'll get psyched out if you look too long."

"Let's just do it," she said.

We hiked back to the canoe and went through all the safety precautions: fully inflating the air bags, making sure the bow and stern ropes were coiled so they wouldn't get tangled in our feet if we capsized. We cinched down our thigh straps and tightened our life jackets.

The entrance to Gabriel's Bend lies at a forty-five-degree angle to the rapid around the tip of an island. You can't see the rapid until you're on top of it, which makes it difficult to line up the canoe. I tried to keep us to the inside of the channel away from the first set of waves, but the current swept us into the middle, right into their path.

"Brace!" I cried.

Cathy laid her paddle flat against the water to stabilize the boat. We plunged into a hole and submarined through the next wave.

"Paddle!"

The canoe labored up the crest and dropped into the next wall. Each wave tossed in another bucketful of water. The pillowed rock loomed ahead.

"Draw right!"

The water-logged canoe barely moved.

"Right! Right! Right!"

We drew hard, cleared the rock by inches, and raced into the light. The canoe was a bathtub of water, tippy with the shifting weight. We turned out of the current with delicate strokes and eased our way toward shore.

"Good job!" I said. "We made it!"

The riverscape below Gabriel's Bend is as stunning as the rapid itself. A wide pool stretches the width of the Haw, rimmed on the upstream side by a low rock wall. Water gushes through the fissures in a thousand rivulets, each with its own arc and timbre. We snugged the boat against the wall and climbed out on the rocks.

I stripped off my wet shirt and let the sun warm my chest. The kayakers lingered at the bottom of the rapid, playing in the curling wave below the pillowed rock. They surfed forward and sideways, rolled upside-down and popped back up. These guys were like river otters, never so happy as when they were in the water.

I unstrapped the cooler from the canoe and carried it onto the rocks. While Cathy sliced apples and cheese, the kayakers pulled off their spray skirts and helmets. Jim passed out cans of beer; the difficult rapids were over.

From our sun-drenched perch, I surveyed the surroundings. Loblolly pines, trunks as thick as temple pillars, commanded the high ground. Boulders spotted with orange and green lichen crowded the riverbed, whitewater dancing in between.

"Man, I love this river," I said. "It's like a good novel. You've got this long buildup to Gabriel's Bend and then this great run out to the end."

Jim frowned. "Did you hear about the reservoir?"

I said I hadn't.

"The Army Corps of Engineers is building a dam about ten miles downstream. It's going to flood every rapid from here to the Steel Bridge—Slippery Ledge, S-Turn, the Pipeline—"

"What for?"

"Flood control for Fayetteville," Jim said. "Another classic boondoggle. They'd never think to move houses away from the river."

I felt suddenly dizzy. All of this—the trees, the rocks, the river itself—was going to disappear under a sheet of muddy brown. *We die. The rivers die. How are we to live?*

"They say it'll be another five years before they close the floodgates," Jim said. "Enjoy it while you can."

"Hell, I'm moving to the mountains," one of the kayakers said. "Enough of this bullshit."

There was always that option. Take it to another town. But I was tired of looking for greener pastures. I liked Durham, and I liked my job. Something would come up no matter where you lived. I was staying here.

We packed up the boats and paddled across the pool. At this water level, we had our choice of routes: straight ahead over Moose Jaw Falls or left through Harold's Tombstone.

Harold's is a dogleg rapid, a narrow slide at the top followed by a sharp right turn. Lurking at the bottom of the slide is a chiseled rock the size and shape of a tombstone. Cathy and I had never made a clean run of this rapid, glancing hard off the rock each time. Our bright red hull bore dents on both sides as reminders. I wasn't eager to add another.

"Which way are we going, Jim?" I asked.

"Best to do Harold's at this level," he said. "Moose Jaw's a five-foot drop."

As we approached the rapid, I reminded Cathy to draw hard right.

"I know, John. That's the fifth time you've told me."

We drifted under a leaning sycamore and started down the chute. The Tombstone rushed toward us, water piling against its face.

"Now!" I yelled.

Cathy stabbed her blade and pulled to the right. I drew hard in the stern. To no avail. We banged against the tombstone and yawed upstream. Violating one of the cardinal rules, I reached out and pushed off the rock with my hand. We were not going to capsize again.

We cleared the rapid and glided to a walk. I clapped my paddle across the gunwales. "We hit that damn thing every time," I said. "You need to draw repeatedly, not just once."

"I drew a bunch of times," Cathy said. "You didn't see it."

I sighed. Maybe that's the way it was going to be with us. We were always going to hit Harold's Tombstone.

The kayakers passed us and went on over Slippery Ledge. Cathy and I followed behind, managing that rapid and the S-Turn without incident.

From here on down, it was a straight shot to the take-out, a quarter mile of foot-high waves known as The Pipeline. Normally, we glided down this section, me ruddering in the stern and letting the current carry us along. This time, I wanted to try something different.

"Let's paddle as fast as we can," I said. "Get up some real speed."

Cathy gave an eager nod.

As we slid into the rapid, I leaned into my stroke. Soon we were going twice the speed of the current, flying past the rips and bubbles. I loved the feel of the wind in my face, the effortless motion of the boat.

"You're doing great!" I hollered.

We paddled hard until the rapids ended. The criss-crossed trusses of the Steel Bridge loomed ahead. Here was another landmark that would disappear when the river was dammed. I would miss it.

We drove the canoe ashore and tossed our paddles on the bank. I gave Cathy a hug. "That was our best run ever," I said.

Jim and his friends were nowhere in sight. We walked up to the bridge for a better view, leaned against the rusted steel trusses. Above the distant rush of water, I heard the muffled shouts of the kayakers upstream, where the river emerged from a tunnel of sycamores.

"Hear that?" I said. "They're playing in the rapids."

Cathy smiled wistfully. None of this was sure to last. But I could ask her to marry me. *Yes,* I thought, *that's what I'll do.*

CHAPTER SEVEN

The Allagash

Daylight warmed the orange fabric of the tent and lured me out of my sleeping bag. Cathy was still asleep, her tousled blonde head turned toward the corner. I unzipped the entry to find last night's toothed silhouette now a ridge of spruce fir. Heron Lake sparkled in the morning sun. The river emerged from beneath the wooden timbers of the Churchill Dam, rippling past the campground with barely a sound.

Damon was already up, staring at the river through wire-rimmed glasses. He stroked his moustache. "Can you believe it?" he said. "The Allagash!"

I shook my head. "Thought we'd never make it."

We'd driven more than a thousand miles to get here, my Capri and Damon's Honda with the canoes on top buffeted by tractor trailers and buses all the way up I-95. We reached the take-out near the Canadian border late on the afternoon of the second day. After leaving Damon's Honda by the river, we crammed in the Capri and drove 150 miles to the put-in, a circuitous route around and through vast swaths of commercial timberland surrounding the waterway.

The narrow band of sky was dimming fast as we tunneled through the forest on a dirt logging road, sixty miles without a house or a sign. I was all but convinced we were lost. Then the lake and river appeared, glowing like polished pewter in the last light of day.

Now, Maggie emerged from her tent with a puckish smile, elbows snugged in tight. "We're here!" she said. Cathy appeared moments later, and together we stood on the bank beaming at the river.

Damon and Maggie were among Cathy's and my best friends, the first couple we had bonded with since getting married. We'd met Damon when we were all at Carolina, and Maggie, when she began dating Damon some years later. Damon was boisterous, intelligent, opinionated to the point of offending some people. His first marriage had ended in divorce, but Cathy and I were hopeful that his relationship with Maggie would work out. She was joyful and spirited, her good humor a balance to Damon's occasional flashes of anger.

Both were canoeists. Maggie was thin, but strong, a competent bow paddler. Damon's sturdy build and athletic conditioning made him a natural in the stern. Together we'd paddled all the local rivers and a handful in the Appalachian Mountains.

It was after one of our trips on the Lower Haw that we came up with the idea for running the Allagash. Here was our chance to explore a legendary river, written about in all the canoeing literature. For Cathy and me, this was very likely our last big canoe trip before we had kids.

The Allagash is one of the few waterways in the East where you can canoe for five or six days without encountering any signs of civilization other than a few log bridges. It's actually a chain of rivers and lakes, running for almost a hundred miles through the north Maine woods. The state of Maine has declared it a Wilderness Waterway, and the federal government a Wild and Scenic River. After negotiating the increasingly crowded rivers in the Southeast, the four of us were eager for a taste of wilderness.

Damon and I untied the canoes from the cartop rack and set them on the bank. I hadn't been canoe camping since Keewaydin, but the old lessons came back—heaviest pack behind the center thwart, lighter pack in front. The gear had changed dramatically since the mid-1960s. Instead of wooden wannigans laden with cans of beef stew, we had aluminum-framed backpacks filled with airy freeze-dried lasagna. The nylon tents and down sleeping bags you could practically hold in one hand. And, of course, we had our ABS canoes, ten to fifteen pounds lighter than the wood and canvas monsters and tougher, as well. No need to worry about breaking a wooden rib out here.

"You take the lead, John," Damon said. "Give us a signal if you see any problems."

There's nothing I like better than paddling a good boat into new water with the sun on my cheek and a light wind ruffling my hair. We launched into the river below Churchill Dam.

The current stayed strong as we rode the blue highway through the forest. We flew past evergreen and birch, the latter's small, heart-shaped leaves fluttering pale side up in the breeze.

A quarter-mile down, we reached the head of Chase Rapids, labeled on the waterway map as a long Class II. I rose up on my knees and scanned the river ahead. There didn't appear to be any major obstacles, just a broad stretch of laughing water. I steered down the middle of the channel until a white roostertail appeared.

"Rock straight ahead," I noted to Cathy. "Go left."

She moved us away with a few quick draws. Sure enough, there was a jagged hunk of granite underneath that tail. Using a common river runner's signal to change direction, I raised my paddle overhead, angled to the left. Damon and Maggie seemed not to notice.

Their canoe hit with a jarring thud and tipped to one side. I thought for sure they were going over, but the canoe rocked back to level. Damon's baritone yell rang out. "Damn it, Maggie, what are you doing?"

I shook my head. "There goes the trip," I said to Cathy.

Maggie's soothing response floated across the water. "I'm sorry, Damon. I didn't see it." She sounded just like my mother, ever the peacemaker, deflecting my father's anger after some upset.

Damon and Maggie focused their attention back on the river, and by the time they pulled abreast, they were both smiling. *This is how they'll do it. This is how relationships survive.*

Damon laughed. "We managed to hit the one rock in the river. How's that for a start?"

"Lucky you fiberglassed that nose," I said.

Damon and I owned identical canoes. Both had come from the same batch of factory seconds with the soft noses. He'd also done his own repairs, but instead of two layers of fiberglass, Damon had lathered on four. That rendered the nose as blunt as a boot heel, not a major problem on the whitewater rivers we paddled where the current pushed us along. But a sharp nose is crucial for a canoe's ability to glide, and I worried what would happen when we hit the Allagash lakes.

The current rippled on below Chase Rapids, carrying us along at a runner's clip. I leaned back and ruddered. No need to paddle. Beneath the hull, a collage of olive, cream, and pink stones raced past. I hadn't seen anything like this since the Chagrin.

A flock of ducks swam upstream along the shore. Gray backs, bronze-crested heads, hooked beaks — these were new to me. As we came abreast, the ducks craned their necks and scooted forward like toy hydroplanes. Mergansers! I laughed at their needless flight. How many canoeists would pass before these ducks understood we were not a threat? Evolution, I mused, had not conditioned them to take a relaxed attitude toward life.

"Hey, guys," Damon called. "How about we smoke a doobie?"

He lifted a plastic baggie and handed it to Maggie. While Damon kept the canoe running straight, she rolled a joint in her lap.

I felt uneasy about getting high on unfamiliar waters, especially out here in the wilderness. Shouldn't we stay alert? What the hell. There weren't supposed to be any more rapids, and we had only a few miles to go.

We drew the canoes close together. Maggie passed the lit joint to Cathy. She took a hit and handed it back to me. My nostrils filled with the pungent odor of marijuana, dashing the scent of the pine woods. I felt instantly dizzy. The Allagash became a carnival ride, our canoes sweeping around the bends as if on rails. Who would ever think we could get away with this!

Within a few miles, the current died as we reached the head of

Lake Umsaskis. The banks retreated to reveal an undulating line of low green hills. Marshmallow clouds floated on the horizon. It was time for lunch.

We lashed the canoes together in the middle of the lake and opened the cooler. Maggie fixed sandwiches and passed them around. "I just can't believe we're out here," Damon said. "This is heaven."

The warmth of the day, the buzz of marijuana, put me in the mood for a nap. I slipped off my sneakers and propped my feet on the center thwart. As the canoes bobbed on the gentle swells, I imagined I was back in Keewaydin. That was a good time. This was better—free of the insecurities of youth, the need to march to the counselor's drum. I was on my own now.

"We should head on before we fall asleep," Damon said. "Map says the campsite is about a mile away."

We picked up our paddles and eased down the lake. The campsite stood on the southern shore at the tip of a rocky peninsula. We beached the canoes and climbed the gentle grade to the clearing beneath the pines. Half-a-dozen empty tent sites and two fire rings had been laid out at opposite ends of the slope. We chose the higher ground and set up our tents.

"That ledge looked like a great place to dive," I said. "Anyone up for a swim?"

Damon announced his intention to join me. I donned my bathing suit and ambled down to the lake.

The ledge stood a dozen feet above the water, facing back down the lake the way we had come. A fleet of canoes appeared in the distance—all of them green with big numbers on the bow. A summer camp.

Damon stood by me as the canoes drew near.

"I hope they're not planning on staying here," I said.

"They're not," Damon answered. "Simple as that."

But the campers came right on shore without a glance in our direction. Eight boys hopped out and scampered across the lower half of the campground. "I got this site," claimed one with long blonde hair. "This one's ours," yelled another.

I approached one of the counselors as he stepped onshore, a twenty-something guy wearing a felt fedora. "Excuse me," I said. "This is our campsite. We've been here for at least an hour."

He offered a sympathetic smile. "These big campsites are meant to be shared. There's not enough on the river for everyone to have their own."

Damon glared at him. "If you're staying, we're moving. Come on, John."

I followed Damon up the hill. He told the women what was going on and started dismantling his tent. "Come on, Maggie. Help me out," he said.

Just then the counselor appeared. "You guys don't have to do this," he said. "We're really not a bad bunch."

We stood silent.

"I can tell you for a fact there's another couple of parties coming along behind us. We camped with a family last night. The dad was nuts, yelling at his kids. You wouldn't want to get stuck with them."

Cathy sighed. "Let's stay here, John. I don't want to pack all this up."

"Yeah, Damon, let's stay here," Maggie said.

I shrugged. Damon's shoulders sagged. "Whatever you guys want," he said.

The counselor headed back down the hill, leaving us staring at the ground.

"Let's bring all our stuff up here," I said. "I'll get some firewood."

"We'll get dinner going," Maggie said.

Damon stood in place, not yet ready to let go of his anger. He turned and pushed the tent stakes back in the ground.

As I combed the fringes of the forest, I kept an ear tuned to the campers.

"Hey, Thompson, check this out. I've got the perfect marshmallow stick."

"Screw you. Mine's better than that."

Just like the kids at Keewaydin.

At dinner, we promised each other we would find our own campsite the following night. Our "wilderness" permit was clear about staying only in designated campgrounds, but the country seemed vast and no one would notice if we ducked off the river somewhere.

Afterward, Cathy rummaged through the container I'd packed with cookwear. "Did you remember to bring the detergent, John?"

"I think I forgot it."

"Do you guys have any?"

Maggie shook her head.

Cathy glanced at the campers. "Maybe they'll have some."

She walked down the hill and introduced herself to the counselor with the felt hat. He reached into a pack and handed her a plastic tube. They struck up a conversation.

Twenty minutes later, Cathy returned, full of information about "Ian." She related that he was a psychology graduate student at Boston College, that he'd started out doing social work, and now took this job as a counselor in the summer. "He went to a canoe camp just like you, John. He's paddled this river before."

I pursed my lips, glanced at this Ian fellow.

The next morning after breakfast, I walked down to the lake to wash the dishes. I found Ian by the shore filling a water jug. We exchanged greetings.

"Hear you paddled this river before," I said.

"About ten years ago."

"See any wildlife?"

"Couple of moose. Had a big bull swim right in front of my canoe."

I expressed surprise, asked him where on the river this had happened.

"I don't remember, but they're all over the place," he said. "Your best chance to see one is to get out on the river before anyone else. Moose like to feed on the aquatic grasses."

I thanked him and hurried back up the hill to tell the others. We broke camp and headed out on the lake.

A cloud front had moved in overnight, rendering the sky, the land, and water in proximate shades of lifeless gray. My mood darkened. I recalled the rainy days at Keewaydin paddling in silence under sullen skies. I scanned the shoreline. Nothing.

Over the course of the morning, Damon and Maggie started to fall behind. They were every bit as strong as Cathy and I, so it had to be the canoe. I eased off my stroke and waited for them to catch up.

"That nose slowing you down?" I asked Damon.

"What do you mean?"

"Your patch job. Kind of fat for lake paddling."

Damon scowled, and I felt stupid for opening my mouth. Dad did this all the time, expressed some pent-up annoyance tinged with sarcasm. I remembered the first time Cathy caught me doing it myself, and said I sounded just like my father. *Not me,* I thought at the time. *I didn't mean it the way he did.*

By late afternoon, we reached Round Pond. Our campsite lay somewhere on the eastern shore at the base of a prominent hill. The map indicated there was a trail behind the campsite leading up to a fire tower. We had intended to stay an extra day so we could hike up to the tower, but it was nowhere in sight. Perhaps it stood on the far side of the hill.

A cavelike opening in the wooded shoreline marked the entrance to the campsite. We beached our canoes and stepped into the shadows. The campsite was much smaller than our last one with a single fire ring and two tent sites. Surely, this was designed for just one group. But who knew what the practice was here? We flipped the canoes over to signify our intention to stay and set up camp.

I picked the tent site closest to the water beneath the sheltering boughs of cedar tree. Cathy scooped up a handful of small brown needles. "Smell these," she said.

I inhaled the scent of Christmas trees, felt the dry, firm ground. "We'll sleep well tonight," I said.

Maggie let out a whoop and I turned to see her wading naked into the lake, her girlish frame hunched to the cold. Damon followed behind, stepping gingerly over the rocky bottom. The sun had broken through the clouds, etching their skin in gold. Damon squeezed some Doctor Bronner's soap into his hand and rubbed it in his crotch.

"Woo hoo!" he said. "That stings."

Cathy and I brought out our sleeping pads and leaned them against the log by the fire ring. I made a miniature teepee out of pencil-thin cedar twigs and poked a burning match in between. As the fire crackled to life, we took off our shoes and snuggled close. This was just how I'd imagined the Allagash to be.

We woke the next morning to a cloudless sky, promising a spectacular view from the fire tower. We ate a leisurely breakfast, then packed a lunch and headed out along the trail behind the campsite. Legions of gray-trunked cedars hunkered in the shadows, giving way to leafy hardwoods as the trail gained elevation. We stopped to pick raspberries beside the trail. Damon lit a joint.

Today I was in the mood for getting high. I marveled at the lacey-winged damselflies lighting on the branches. We hiked for a few minutes, then stopped to pick more berries. Started and stopped again.

The trail leveled out as we reached the top of the hill. Sunlight shone in a clearing. A metal structure lay on the ground with a crumpled cabin at the end—the fire tower.

In stunned silence, we walked into the clearing to find a trio of workmen eating lunch beside a tracked vehicle. I asked what had happened to the tower.

The workman lowered his thermos. "Blew it up."

"When?"

"Last week."

JOHN MANUEL   113

I threw my hands atop my head.

"Why'd you do that?" Maggie said.

"Department of Forestry transferred the waterway to Parks and Lands. Didn't want the liability."

The men continued eating as if this kind of thing happened every day. I examined the cement footings that once anchored the tower. The metal braces were charred and twisted.

"So what are you doing now?" I asked.

The man wiped his sleeve across his mouth. "Puttin' it back."

"Why?"

"Parks and Lands wants it so's people like you can enjoy the view."

I turned to the others, stoned smirks spreading across their faces. "Nice to know bureaucracy is alive and well in the wilderness," Damon said.

"Come back next week," the man said. "Should be up."

We walked a dozen yards down the trail, then fell down laughing. We rolled across the ground until our faces were covered with dirt.

"Tell me this isn't real," Maggie said.

Damon chortled. "No one's ever gonna believe this."

With no other destination in mind, we decided to eat lunch where we lay. We managed to get the food in our mouths, but every few seconds, one of us would mimic the workmen's lines and we would burst into laughter. Pieces of tuna fish littered the ground.

Back in camp, we stood around the dormant fire, uncertain of what to do with the rest of our day. Damon gave Maggie a sly look.

"I think Maggie and I are going to take a nap," he said.

Cathy and I decided to do the same. We slipped into our orange cocoon and wiggled out of our clothes. As I rolled into her embrace, laughter erupted from the other tent, Damon's voice going high and low. "What're you doing? Puttin' it back."

We emerged for dinner, sharing another intimate evening by the campfire, then returned to our tents for the night.

In the morning, Maggie rapped on our tent. Damon was sick. He'd thrown up several times and was running a slight fever. I suggested we get help. Maggie demurred. "This always happens to him on vacation. He gets stressed out at work, and when he relaxes, his body needs to purge itself." Cathy and I exchanged crestfallen glances. We'd hoped to make it to Allagash Falls that day.

"You guys go ahead," Maggie said. "We'll catch up with you tomorrow."

I offered a mild protest, but in truth, I was grateful for the chance for Cathy and me to be on our own. I wouldn't be tempted to muddy my head with pot. Best of all, we could get out on the river early.

At the end of Round Pond, we slipped back into the serpentine channel of the Allagash. The current pushed us along like an old friend. Along the bottom, long strands of yellow-green grass wavered downstream. We rounded the bend, and my dream finally came true.

The moose stood in midstream, antlers swaying back and forth as he worked the grasses loose. I whispered to Cathy not to move, slipped a camera out of my pack and screwed on a telephoto lens. I held my breath, waited for just the right moment. He thrust his head out of the water and stared at the canoe, silver droplets streaming from his muzzle. I snapped the picture, wound and snapped another.

We glided so close that I started to worry. What if he decided to charge? But he acted as if he had seen plenty of canoeists before. He waded ashore with an unhurried gate, stared at us one last time, then slipped between the alders.

Cathy turned around, beaming. She knew how much this meant to me, how seeing these animals in the wild reaffirmed my faith in the world. Best of all, we'd witnessed the moose together. We had a story of our own.

With the sun straight overhead, we stopped for lunch on an island in midstream. Cathy peeled an orange and fed it to me. We took off our clothes—she pale as a Degas nude—and tiptoed into the river. I breaststroked into deep water and spun in slow circles. The water lifted my genitals with a silken hand. I closed my eyes and floated on my back. Small waves kissed my cheek.

Late in the afternoon, we reached the portage for Allagash Falls. The river offered no hint of what was to come, disappearing around the bend as placid as a millpond. But I could hear the rumble of falling water, feel its tremor in the ground.

The trail emerged at the head of the falls, a blinding white cataract tumbling over dark sheaves of slate. Boys in swimsuits were scaling the rocks on the far side of the river. I recognized the one with the long blonde hair.

"Look who's here," I said.

Cathy sighed. "Another night with the campers."

We followed the trail to the base of the falls, passing half-a-dozen occupied campsites. An elderly couple sat tending their fire. A man tossed a frisbee with his kids. There would be no solo camping tonight.

Ian sat at a picnic table mixing a bowl of flour and water. I was surprised at how happy I was to see him. I strode up and patted him on the back, told him of our sighting.

"You were right, man," I admitted. "The secret is getting out early."

Ian invited us to share the campsite with him and the boys. Cathy and I exchanged glances.

"Why not?" I said.

We set up our tent and donned our swimsuits, eager to wash off the day's sweat. Boys were lined up on a ledge, jumping into the foamy water below the falls. I thought of the time diving off the bluffs at Obabika Lake. I missed that playful one-upmanship, the exhilaration of letting go despite your fear.

"Mind if I join you?" I said.

The last boy turned around. "Hey, Dane. It's those same people."

I stepped to the edge and looked down. It had been more than a decade since I'd jumped from this height. I let out a whoop and dove. The black water rushed toward me, exploding in a fizz of bubbles.

Cathy jumped in after me, and together with the boys, we tried to swim to the base of the falls. I flailed my arms, but the current was too strong. One by one, we gave up and drifted downstream.

Back at the campsite, Ian bent over the fire, stirring a pot of stew while keeping an eye on the biscuits in the reflector oven. Cathy and I gladly accepted his invitation to dinner. We were starting to feel like family.

I dug my tin plate out of my pack and stood in line with the campers. I might as well have been fourteen again, peering around their shoulders, worried that I wouldn't get enough. Then that first mouthful of stew went down, and my anxiety disappeared. I leaned back against the tree and watched the feathered clouds in our small patch of sky change from pink to orange to gray.

Ian lit the Coleman lantern and hung it on a nail. He directed a group of boys to gather the dishware and followed them down the darkening trail to the river. The three who remained at the picnic table broke out a deck of cards.

"Wanna join us?" a boy named T.J. said.

"I'm not much of a poker player," I said. "Mind if we sit and watch?"

"Sure, come on."

The game was five-card draw with matchsticks as money. A few hands in, it became clear that blonde-headed Dane was the master at this game. He upped the ante regardless of what he was holding, fixing the other boys with a cold stare. Chase and T.J. folded every time.

Dane scooped up his winnings, adding to his already considerable pile. T.J. reached for Dane's discarded hand. "Let's see your cards."

Dane grabbed them up. "Screw you!"

"Man, you were bluffing!"

"That's for me to know and you to find out."

T.J. tossed his matchsticks on the table. "I quit."

"Me, too," Chase said.

An old anger welled inside me. I remembered this game, being bluffed into submission by that asshole Shephard, thinking that people like him would always come out on top. I wanted to grab the cards out of Dane's hand and expose him as the loser I knew he was. But I stayed quiet.

"How do you guys like camp?" Cathy asked.

"It's okay."

"It's a lot of paddling."

Dane sniffed. "I think it sucks. My Dad sent me here so he could hang out with his new girlfriend."

Then, Dane started sweeping up the spilled flour on the table with a playing card, forming it into two lines. He took a dollar bill from his pocket, rolled it up and stuck it in his nose.

Chase guffawed. "Are you crazy?"

"Do it," T.J. said.

Dane stared at me, waiting. I'd never been challenged by a bitter fourteen-year-old, never imagined a boy his age could know about cocaine. It wasn't my place to discipline him, nor was it Cathy's. We glanced at each other, waited for him to make the next move.

"Just kidding," Dane said.

Ian returned and put the dishes on the table. "Okay, guys, time for bed."

The boys shuffled back to their tents. Ian asked us if he should leave the lantern on.

"No, thanks," I said. "We're heading off to bed."

Ian shut off the light and the world went black. Like a flashgun had popped in my face, I saw an after-image of Dane, staring at me with that dollar bill up his nose. I reached for Cathy's hand under the table. She gave me a squeeze. I knew what she was thinking. We'd been married now for two years. The time was coming soon. The thought of having a baby, any baby, was scary enough. But what if we were dealt a losing hand? What if we got a Dane?

In the morning, we walked to the head of the falls to wait for

Damon and Maggie. The other parties were packing up their canoes and paddling downstream. We would see no moose today.

Damon and Maggie arrived around noon. Damon had fully recovered and both were in good spirits. We ate a quick lunch by the falls and headed for the take-out at Twin Brook.

The roar of the falls faded behind, replaced by the distant whine of a chainsaw. The sound grew louder at every turn, accompanied now by the growl of a bulldozer. I recalled from the Allagash brochure that the "Wilderness Waterway" extended only five hundred feet back from the river; beyond that, commercial logging was permitted. The importance of this arrangement was now becoming clear. This so-called wilderness was more illusion than fact. Reality lay beyond the thin veil of trees.

Mile by mile, the river grew wider and shallower. I spotted one of the groups that had set off before us. They were out of their boats, dragging them across a gravel bar. Having spent many a summer day poling my canoe down the ankle-deep Chagrin, I'd become somewhat of an expert at reading shallow water. I knew at a glance the difference between two inches of water and three, where my boat would hang up and where it could sneak through.

I stood up and scanned the river. "Over there," I pointed. "Along the bank."

We passed the older couple who had been at the campsite, hard aground and panting in the afternoon sun. Farther along, we passed the family as they squabbled over how to pull the boats. The river was played out, and so were we.

A cluster of parked cars appeared on the left bank.

"There's the take-out," Damon called. "We've made it."

We beached the canoes and exchanged high fives. All in all, it had been a wonderful vacation. We'd survived with no guide to plan our trip, lead us down the river, or mediate disputes.

We unloaded the gear and crammed it in the hatchback of the Honda. Damon and I tied the boats on the roof rack. Now, for the awful drive back to the put-in. I scrunched in the back seat with Cathy and leaned my head against the window. A short time after we reached the paved road, I fell asleep.

The rumble of wheels on gravel stirred me awake. I glanced out the window at the blurred canopy of trees. The car slowed to a halt.

"Canoes are sliding off," Damon announced. "We need to retie the ropes."

I hauled myself out and helped Damon shove the canoes back on the rack. I picked at one of the knots, but it wouldn't budge.

"Thing's stuck," I said.

"You need to retie it."

I tried but couldn't loosen the knot. "The canoes aren't going anywhere," I said. "Even if the gunwale slides off the edge, the rope will keep them on."

Damon frowned.

"I'm telling you," I insisted, "they aren't coming off."

We climbed back in the car and headed on through the forest. Finally, we broke into the clearing. There was Churchill Dam and my Capri. We were all cheering when Damon swung into the parking lot, hit the pothole, and skidded to a halt. A shadow descended, followed by a deafening whack.

For an instant, no one spoke. The windows on my side of the car crackled like ice in a glass of water. Beneath the canoe that hung off the roof, I could see the Allagash rippling into the forest, fragmenting into a thousand pieces until it was nothing more than a blur of light.

CHAPTER EIGHT

The Rocky

In Chatham County, North Carolina, the land lies in gentle folds, pale green pastures rising to forested ridgelines. Down in the swales, farmers grow the grass long to slow the runoff from the rains. But the water's will is insistent, and as it works its way into the wooded valley, it parts the soil and lays bare the bedrock, giving birth to the Rocky River.

More hissing stream than river, the Rocky is unnavigable for most of the year. A long-legged girl could wade across the channel without getting her shorts wet. Snakes sun unmolested on the rocks. But for a few days each spring, torrential rains swell the Rocky to twice her normal size. Canoeists descend on the river from all across the piedmont, filling the air with shouts and laughter. The orgy lasts a day, maybe two; then the water drops, and the boaters leave. The Rocky whispers alone again.

⊹

Cathy came out of the bathroom holding the pregnancy kit. "It's positive," she said.

For a long minute, neither of us spoke. We'd been trying to get pregnant for almost a year, but now that it had happened, we thought of all the reasons this wasn't a good time. Cathy would have to cancel her family planning workshop in Nairobi. And we could forget about that canoe trip to the Boundary Waters.

"I guess there's never going to be a perfect time," Cathy said. "We just have to accept that things are going to change."

Her body was the first thing to be transformed. Cathy lost her tapered waist and slender arms. But her face flushed with expectant pride, and even her swollen belly struck me as beautiful. Until she began to feel pain.

At sixteen weeks, Cathy's ligaments ached and her fundus seemed much larger than normal. We went to the hospital for a routine check-up. The doctor ran his ultrasound wand across her belly and stared at the monitor. Two fuzzy shapes appeared, facing each other like yin and yang.

"You've got twins," Dr. Sims said. "Boys."

My stomach dropped. One child was what we had planned. One child I could handle. Two meant a total loss of freedom. Twins owned their parents.

"There is something else going on here," Dr. Sims observed.

He recentered the wand.

"This fetus is smaller than his brother. It could have something to do with your swelling. The amniotic fluid may not be circulating properly. We're going to have to watch that."

In the weeks that followed, Cathy's belly continued to swell. Her skin stretched so tight it hurt her to touch it. One twin remained normal sized; the other hardly grew. As twenty weeks approached, we faced a crucial juncture. Beyond that time an abortion was illegal.

One more time we looked at the images on the screen. "My guess is that the smaller twin will die before it comes to term," Dr. Sims said. "In that case, it will kill the other one, too."

The words seemed to come from far away. My thoughts drifted to our last canoe trip on the Rocky River.

"Are you paying attention, John?" the doctor asked. "I see this glazed look in your eye."

I struggled to regain focus. "Yeah, I'm listening."

He turned back to the monitor. "Cathy, your fundus is much larger than it should be at this stage. If the swelling continues, it will start to affect your breathing. That could be dangerous."

Cathy spoke in her professional voice. "What can we do?"

The doctor shook his head. "The only way to eliminate the threat is to terminate the pregnancy. But that's a decision for you all to make."

❦

The spring before Cathy became pregnant, the rains fell hard in the Carolina piedmont. Word from the paddle shops was that the Rocky River should be runnable. I called Damon and asked if he and Maggie could join us.

"As long as we take your car," he joked.

Damon had forgiven me for not retying that rope. He and Maggie had driven the entire way back to North Carolina with shattered windows. But the car was now repaired, Damon and Maggie had gotten married, and we were back to running rivers together. They agreed to meet us at the 902 bridge.

The four of us had run the Rocky once before, several years past. My memory of the rapids was vague, the others' non-existent.

"All I remember is that broken dam about halfway down," Damon said as we stood on the bridge.

I glanced at the muddy torrent surging around the pylons below us. "I can tell you it's at least a foot higher than the last time," I said.

At the put-in, Cathy slipped on her paddling gloves and playfully rocked the boat. I was surprised at how relaxed she was, trusting that we could face whatever came along. I, for one, was nervous.

"You guys stay close," I said to Damon and Maggie.

As we shoved off the bank, I rose up on my knees. The current drew us toward the bend and the rush of falling water.

"Draw left!" I said, as the rapid came into view.

We angled toward a narrow opening between two mossy boulders. Our approach was good, but as we dropped down the curling tongue, the Explorer hit a submerged rock and shuddered to a crawl. I gave a push and we slid right off, nothing but a little red paint left behind.

I loved this boat. After seven years, the bottom was streaked and gouged in a hundred places, but the skin had never cracked. I'd re-fiberglassed the nose several times, but that was to be expected. You couldn't hit Harold's Tombstone head on and not expect to pay the price.

The Rocky twisted through the forest, never affording a distant view. I tried to anticipate the size of the unseen rapids by the sound—a hiss, a rush, a roar.

Damon and Maggie followed close behind, his commands echoing my own. Every now and then I heard his basso reassurance: "Doing great, Maggie. Doing great."

A wall of trees appeared in midstream, their trunks seeming to rise straight out of the water. Something wasn't right about that.

"Here's the dam!" I realized. "Get to shore!"

We ran the canoes onto the bank and tied the bow lines to the alders. I clambered across the rocks to a spot below the dam. Cathy, Maggie, and Damon followed.

The last time we were here, the old stone structure was clearly visible, water funneling through a break on one side. Now, it was submerged beneath a maelstrom of yard-high waves that ran on for fifty yards. *"Intense, powerful rapids requiring precise boat handling in turbulent water...May feature large or unavoidable waves or holes...Risk of injury to swimmers is moderate to high..."* This was the very definition of a Class IV rapid.

"I think we need to walk this one," I said.

Damon nodded. "Good call."

I hated to bypass a rapid; there was always a way down. In fact, I could see the route to take. If I were paddling solo, I'd probably chance it. But two of us together would definitely swamp. I hopped back upstream and waited by the canoe. Cathy picked her way slowly through the rocks.

I grabbed the canoe and started dragging it. "Come on, let's get going," I said.

"Take it easy," Cathy snapped. "I'm trying to get there."

I stopped pulling. *When you get scared, you turn inward and cold. That helps no one.*

We set the canoes on the rocks below the dam and talked about what to do next. I could see another big drop ahead, but the banks were tangled with driftwood. We couldn't put in any farther downstream, and there was no place to pull over and scout. We'd have to run this one blind.

Back in the canoe, we approached the rapid; I rose up on my knees trying to see the bottom.

"Brace!"

We plunged into the hole, the bow disappearing into the steep wave on the downstream side.

"Paddle!"

We labored forward, the boat suddenly heavy and unresponsive. "Eddy out," I said. "We've got to bail!"

I scanned the shore for slack water. Nothing. We'd have to hold on to whatever we could. We swung the boat around and drove it against the bank. Cathy grabbed a branch. I started bailing.

⌁

We scheduled the abortion for the following week. The nurse ushered Cathy into a private room. There was a plastic chair in the corner, a bed, and a window looking out over the tops of the loblolly pines. I picked up a magazine and tried to read.

Dr. Sims arrived and explained the procedure. He would give Cathy an injection of prostaglandin to induce labor. Contractions would begin in two to three hours.

"I'll be doing my rounds, but the nurse will call me when the time comes," he said. He gave me a cool glance and left the room.

I despised this hospital with its airless rooms, its sick and dying patients. I sat on the bed and held Cathy's hand, got up and stared out the window.

"Listen, I'm going out for some lunch," I said. "I'll be back in an hour."

Cathy sighed. She could see I was no good at this. I took her "okay" as a sign of assent and hurried out the door.

Downtown Chapel Hill looked just as it did the day I arrived. Students strolled the brick sidewalks in cut-off jeans and flip-flops. But their carefree laughter rang flat. Life could turn on them at any moment. They had no clue how they would react. Some would be heroes and others cowards.

I ate a hamburger on Franklin Street and headed back to the hospital. As I stepped off the elevator, the nurse hurried past.

"She's already in labor," she said.

I hurried into the room to find Dr. Sims leaning over the bed. Cathy cried out in pain.

"You're going to need to step outside," the doctor said.

I waited in the hall. Cathy's cries pierced through the soothing reassurances of the doctor and nurse. After a prolonged silence, Sims emerged carrying a plastic bucket.

"Do you want to see?" he asked.

The boys lay on their sides in a pool of clear liquid and blood. Their arms were bent, hands curled as if holding something—a blanket, a paddle? Their journey on earth was over. I went in to see Cathy.

✦

When it comes to who calls out the obstacles in tandem canoeing, there are no hard-and-fast rules. The bow paddler is in the best position to see the oncoming rapids, but the more experienced canoeist, usually seated in the stern, may have the better read. What matters is that you stick with your established procedure.

We were within sight of the 902 bridge when I saw the rock in midstream, a flat-topped boulder partially hidden by a pillowed wave. We could have dodged it easily if I'd called it out, but I decided to keep quiet. I was tired of always being the one to give orders, to be on the lookout for trouble. I wanted to test Cathy, see how long it would take her to react.

We closed in on the rock. Ten yards, nine, eight...Cathy paddled straight ahead.

"Draw right!" I yelled, too late.

We hit just behind the bow and swung sideways to the current. Water surged over the upstream gunwale. Cathy tumbled into the river. I leaned away from the rolling hull and found the rock high and dry. As the boat tipped sideways, I hoisted myself onto it and watched the disaster unfold.

The canoe held rigid at first, the upturned hull cupped against the force of the river. It lasted for perhaps three seconds. With the sound of kindling split over the knee, the wooden gunwales snapped. The hull collapsed and wrapped itself around the rock.

Damon and Maggie raced past, headed after Cathy. Her hips bounced to the surface as she struck the submerged rocks—one, two, three times. There was nothing I could do. I stood untouched on my little island. I could stay there as long as I wanted.

Fifty yards downstream, Cathy dragged herself ashore. Damon and Maggie pulled up and checked to see that she was all right. Then they got out of their canoe and hauled it upstream until they were directly across from me.

"We'll ferry across," Damon yelled.

They paddled against the current, angling into the eddy behind me. Damon motioned for me to get in. I could not bring myself to leave. I yanked hard on one of the ropes, but the canoe wouldn't budge.

"Let's go," Damon said. "You won't be able to free it until the river drops."

I stepped into the boat and squatted behind the center thwart. As Damon and Maggie paddled downstream, I gripped the gunwales with both hands.

Cathy huddled on shore, rubbing her bloodied leg. "I'm all right," she said as I climbed out of the canoe. "Banged up my stupid knee."

"Can you walk?" I asked. "It's only a little way."

She glanced at the bridge, nodded her head. I held out a gloved hand.

Two days later, Cathy and I came back for the canoe. We waded into the now subdued waters and peeled the canoe off the rock. We dragged it through the woods and hoisted it atop the car where it sat like a ruptured red banana.

"It's ruined," I said, and Cathy agreed.

But ABS plastic has a remarkable "memory." We set the boat on sawhorses and weighed the ends down with cinder blocks. Over the course of several days, the hull regained its shape, better than I'd ever have imagined. I bought new gunwales and thwarts, screwed them to the hull, and sanded and varnished them smooth. When it was all done, the canoe still bore a wrinkle around the middle, a reminder of our past. But it paddled straight and true.

CHAPTER NINE

The Chattooga

On Valentine's Day, with a clear winter light gilding the pines outside the hospital window, Cathy gave birth to an eight-pound boy. We named him Jackson, in part because of my memories of my father calling me that when I was young and he in a happy mood. Dad didn't like our choice. When Cathy and I returned to Gates Mills that summer, he mumbled something about giving our son a "Negro name."

"You don't ever remember calling me 'Jackson'?" I asked.

No response. I fought back the tears. Dad was upset that I hadn't named my son "John," as at least five generations of Manuel men had done before. I was intent on breaking that tradition, just as I was determined to treat my son "better." I was going to hold him at every opportunity, sing to him, and most of all make him laugh.

For Jackson I played the funny man, popping up from behind

couches, putting grapes in my eyes. I couldn't get enough of his enormous smile.

As soon as my son could hold himself upright, I hoisted him on my shoulders and carried him into the woods and fields around our house in Durham. I pointed out the hawk circling overhead, the rabbit frozen in the corner of the yard. His small hands pounding on my head told me he'd seen them.

I dreamed of the day when I could take Jackson out in the canoe. I'd bring him along step by step, show him how to hold the paddle and read the rapids. We'd become a real team, paddling all the rivers together. When the time came that he wanted to paddle on his own, I wouldn't hold him back.

To be able to spend more time at home, I quit my job in Raleigh and took one with a new non-profit organization in Research Triangle Park, just down the road from Durham. My job was to promote energy conservation, solar and wind power. I wasn't saving rivers per se, but it was all connected—the energy we consumed, the pollution we spewed into the air that fell back to earth as acidic rainfall and dust.

The first day, I strode into work and shook hands with my new officemate. Keith's wavy, dark hair and beard, his burly build and piercing blue eyes reminded me of Jim East. Looks were not all they had in common.

"Are you a canoeist?" I asked, glancing at the photos on the wall.

"Every chance I get."

I said that I canoed, as well, but hadn't been on the water since the birth of my son the year before.

I paused before the photo of two men in a canoe, buried up to their chests in whitewater. "Where's this one taken?"

"Devil's Kitchen on the Maury River."

"You must be pretty good," I said.

"I paddle with a bunch of guys who spend as much time in the river as they do out. We just like to have fun. You ought to come with us on our next trip. We're headed for Section III of the Chattooga."

The Southern Appalachians give rise to hundreds of rivers. The ancient tree-covered peaks wring the moisture out of the weather systems rolling eastward from Canada, the Pacific and the Gulf of Mexico. The rainfall gathers in clear, tumbling streams, strings of diamonds set in forests of jade.

By the time they are called rivers, these waters have lost their luster. They are sullied with sediment from man's incessant digging, roads chiseled along their banks, dams blocking their flow. But not the Chattooga.

Running fifty miles through valley and gorge, the Chattooga has only a handful of bridge crossings, no riverside development, and is undammed before reaching Lake Tugaloo in the Georgia foothills. Like the Allagash, it has been declared a Federal Wild and Scenic River. Those who've made the long climb out of the gorge know its wildness is no façade.

Guidebooks divide the Chattooga River into four sections. Section III is the gold standard for tandem canoeists, a thirteen-mile run with named rapids around every other bend. There are more than a dozen Class IIIs, three Class IVs, and then the last one, a Class V, aptly named Bull Sluice.

Years before Keith's invitation, Cathy and I had canoed this section with Damon and Maggie. We flew down the river, wide-eyed and laughing, running every rapid except the last. My wife and friends took one look at Bull Sluice with its narrow, twisting channel and boat-eating hydraulic and gladly followed the path to the parking lot. I wavered on the bank for half an hour, torn between the desire to confront this monster and to stay away. Visions of Carrie McCune being hauled from the millrace flashed in my mind. I walked away with slumped shoulders and a migraine headache.

Keith and his friends waited at the Burger King parking lot in Chapel Hill. They seemed like a friendly bunch — George, Michael, Roger, and Keith's wife, Karen. We piled into Keith's van, drove five hours to South Carolina, and set up camp in the dark.

As I lay in my sleeping bag, sandwiched between snoring strangers, my thoughts flew home to Cathy and Jackson. This was the first night I'd been away from home since our son's birth. I would especially miss Cathy not being with me on the river. She was nursing Jackson and wouldn't have been able to come even if she'd wanted. But motherhood had bred a newfound caution in her, as fatherhood had in me. You look at rapids differently once you've had a child.

"Be safe and have fun with your friends," she had told me, as she cradled Jackson in the rocking chair. "I'm happy to stay at home."

Keith was the first one out of his tent in the morning. He fired up his Coleman gas stove and boiled water for coffee. He cooked bacon and eggs and handed them on paper plates to his five groggy companions.

"You're my hero, Keith," Michael said. "If it were left to me, I'd be having toothpaste for breakfast."

"Eat up and get your gear in the van," Keith said. "I'd like to be out of here by nine."

An hour later, we all crowded in the van and drove to the Forest Service parking lot at the trailhead to Earl's Ford. I'd forgotten about the long, steep path to the river with its parade of humans struggling with boats above their heads. I preferred to drag the Explorer as I used to do my Grumman canoe. The well-worn roots and rounded pebbles wouldn't hurt this thing, and I'd have some strength left when I got to the river.

The Chattooga sparkled in the morning sunlight. Ale-colored water flowed over a sandy bottom flecked with mica. I set the canoe on a sandbar and went through the usual preparations: clipping the throw bag and bailer to the rear seat, and the dry bag with my change of clothes to the thwart. I fastened my helmet and gloves, picked up my paddle, and glanced at my tripmates.

Keith and Karen in the yellow canoe were ready to go. Both short and stocky, dressed in paddling jackets and leggings, this husband-and-wife team looked like they were born to canoe. Karen pointed each item out as Keith recited them off his mental checklist. I could learn a thing or two from him.

George, meanwhile, walked around the beat-up red canoe he dubbed "the Freighter," trying to figure out where to stick his cooler. He'd won me over on the drive down with his big laugh and self-deprecating humor. His bright eyes and pointed goatee gave him a sly look; friends called him "the Wolfman." Each trip he wore a new item of clothing with a self-referential moniker. Today's was a T-shirt with the Pillsbury character and the line "Call me Doughboy."

George would be paddling the Freighter with Michael. Eventually.

Six foot two and built like Superman, Michael seemed paralyzed by the decision over which of his several changes of clothes to bring on the river. For minutes at a time, he'd stare at an individual item as if it might speak to him.

I twisted my paddle in the sand. The sun was already above the ridgeline. At this rate, we wouldn't get to Bull Sluice before evening. I didn't know if I would have the courage to run it, but I was in a hurry to find out. And where the hell was my bowman?

"Hey, Keith, have you seen Roger?" I asked.

"He probably forgot something. He'll show up eventually."

By all rights, Roger should have been the most organized of all of us. A successful city planner, a father of three, and member of the local school board, he made a living advising others on how to conduct their affairs. But when it came to organizing himself for a camping trip, he was utterly inept.

At length, Roger emerged from the trail, eyes downcast. "I think I forgot my life jacket. Would anyone happen to have a spare?"

Keith rolled his eyes and threw him the keys to the van. "There's one in the back. Did you bring a paddle?"

"No."

"Jesus Christ, Roger. What *did* you remember?"

Half an hour later, Roger returned with life jacket and paddle. He offered me a sheepish smile. "Keith says you and me are together."

"Do you mind taking bow?" I asked.

"Works fine for me."

After Roger got himself settled, we pushed off the sandbar and rode the gentle current around the bend. Section III starts with a mile of smooth water, but I always feel a drumbeat of fear. Once around that first bend, there's no turning back. There are no roads or houses for the next thirteen miles, and if for any reason you have to get off the river, you face a long hike out. This was not a run where I wanted to be paired with a stranger, but there seemed to be no choice.

"War Woman coming up," Keith called.

War Woman drops in two stages over a yard-high ledge. The second drop must be run at an angle to avoid a rock at the bottom, but it's nothing a decent paddler can't manage. As we slid over the first ledge, I called out for a right-hand draw. Roger hesitated.

"Right!" I said.

Roger made a feeble stab. Too late. We glanced off the rock and yawed hard to the side.

"Come on, man!"

"Sorry! Sorry!" he insisted.

This was bad. If we had trouble on War Woman, what would happen at Dick's Creek, Second Ledge, and Bull Sluice? I missed not having Cathy in the bow. She was strong and quick. Whatever I might say to her about paddling, she knew not to take offense.

Beyond War Woman, the current slowed. Sunlight flashed off the rippling water. The air lay warm and still. High on the ridgetop, leaves fluttered in a silent breeze.

Suddenly, a gunshot rang out downstream. Keith stopped paddling. "What the hell was that?"

"Sounded like a .22," I said.

The Chattooga was made famous as the site where John Boorman filmed the 1972 classic *Deliverance*. I knew better than to think that this river was actually prowled by sadistic rednecks waiting to sodomize hapless boaters. Still, as we drew closer, I could see that the man in the coveralls standing on the bank was most definitely not an actor. And the pistol he held was not a toy.

Keith offered a solemn nod, to which the man responded with a barely noticeable jerk of his blue-capped head. He stared into the water, looking at what, I couldn't tell.

"How ya doin' this morning?" George called.

"Awright."

"What're you up to?"

"Tryin to shoot me some fish."

"Having any luck?"

"Seen a few. Can't seem to hit 'em."

Shooting fish? I cringed in disgust. But George carried on as if he encountered such people every day.

"I hear shock waves'll stun fish. If you graze 'em with a bullet, do they float to the top?"

The man drew a hand over his grizzled chin. "Well, there's them that do and them that don't."

George nodded. "Well, have a good day!"

Around the next bend, we circled the boats. Karen broke into a huge grin. "Are you kidding me?" she said. "That guy was right out of central casting."

"Weee! Weee! Squeal like a pig," Michael said, parroting *Deliverance*'s famous line.

George dropped into a lower register. "Well, there's them that do and them that don't."

I felt the morning's tension flee. I was back on the water on a sunny day.

In the second mile, we came upon a jumble of giant rock slabs thrust from the riverbed at severe angles. The Appalachians are among the world's oldest mountains, formed eons ago by the repeated collisions of the North American, Eurasian, and African continents. The violence of those events is hard to imagine, as subdued as the Appalachians are today. But there is no denying that something cataclysmic had happened here. We whispered as we glided beneath the canted slabs, as if too loud a voice might call them down on our canoes. I snapped a picture of the river gorge behind me, then slid the camera back in the dry bag.

The current picked up speed, running us along the bank and its leafy wall of alder bushes and mountain laurel. I loved the sensation of whisking down a gentle grade, paddle held just so to keep the stern in line.

The river stilled and widened. Through the trees, I glimpsed a waterfall tumbling down a sidestream. I was heartened until I realized this was the marker for Dick's Creek Ledge.

Dick's Creek Ledge is not the most dangerous rapid on Section III, but it is the hardest to run cleanly in a tandem canoe. The ledge drops seven feet in two stages, the first a steep slide into a small pool. The current races across the pool, only to pile up against a humpbacked rock. A thin sheen of water pours over the rock, not enough to float a canoe. The rest is deflected to one side down a chute exactly the width of a canoe. To successfully run the rapid, paddlers must hug the outside edge of the top slide. As they speed towards the rock, they must execute a forty-five degree turn, banking off the watery pillow and riding down the chute. The complexity of this rapid demands that it be scouted.

We beached our canoes on the lip of the ledge, worn smooth and round as the back of a whale. Keith pointed out the route, telling Karen she needed to make a "fierce" right-hand draw to avoid the pillowed rock.

Karen frowned. "I'll do a draw. I don't know how *fierce* it'll be."

As the rest of us watched from the ledge, Keith and Karen paddled into the still water above. Keith rose on his knees to line the boat up. They rode down the slide and into the pool. Keith barked, "Now!" and Karen planted her paddle. The canoe jumped to the right, banked off the pillowed rock, and rode down the chute on a level plane.

I turned to Roger. "Did you see how they did that?"

"I think so."

"You need to do a solid draw."

"Right. Right."

As we paddled upstream, I glanced over my shoulder, keeping my eye on the V of flowing water that disappeared over the first drop. I turned the boat and paddled to the edge. The current grabbed hold, shot us across the pool and toward the pillowed rock. I backwatered hard.

"Draw right!"

The canoe turned as if on rails and dropped into the chute. I was marveling at our success when the boat bumped the edge of the chute and flipped. Face and hands pressed to the rock, I slid down the chute, trapped underneath the canoe and splashed to a halt at the base of the ledge. Two hard kicks and my legs came free of the thigh straps. I stood up in the waist-deep water yards away from Keith and Karen's canoe.

THE CHATTOOGA

"You guys all right?" Keith asked.

Roger looked shell-shocked, his rain suit plastered to his body. "A little banged up," he said, "But I'll survive."

"John?"

I averted my eyes. "Fine." I didn't know what had just happened, but it must have been Roger's fault. This had the makings of a disaster.

Not wanting to repeat our mishap, George and Michael decided to take a "cheat route" over the ledge. They lined the Freighter up to the outside of the V and ran aground in shallow water. Neither wanted to get his feet wet, so they inched down the slide by rocking the boat forward.

"Jesus Christ, guys, get out of the fucking boat!" Keith yelled.

George paused in his rocking. "Never disturb the Doughboy in the midst of his training."

Minutes later, they slid to a halt in the lower pool. I was offended that they had "successfully" run the rapid in such a cowardly fashion. Then George and Michael raised their arms in mock victory, and Keith and Karen broke into applause. I finally realized this wasn't a game of one-upmanship. These guys were here to have fun. And I wanted to be part of it.

My father knew about this—the elixir of friendship, of not taking yourself too seriously. Every summer of my early childhood, he and my mother had hosted a boating party on the Chagrin River. They established a theme—pirates, Vikings, Anthony and Cleopatra on the Nile—and invited everyone they knew with a craft that would float. People dressed in costume, adorned their boats, and launched into the river below our house. Here came Mr. and Mrs. Williams in horned helmets, paddling a canoe with a soaring papier mâché prow. And there was the Hildt's raft, made of doors strapped to fifty-gallon drums. Above it all I could hear my father's guffaw, a falsetto burst with a bass undertone. My mother answered with her high, clear laughter, her eyes squinted shut.

I viewed this merriment from year to year standing on the bank under the watchful eye of a babysitter. I was too young to be on the river by myself or with my sister, Susie. But I vowed that someday I would have my own boating party. I would find my own voice.

Beyond Dick's Creek, the hills that stood back from the river's edge suddenly loomed high and close. Dark spears of hemlock mingled with the paler crowns of poplar and oak. The river slowed and tapered, gathering itself for a charge through the canyon known as The Narrows.

The entrance to The Narrows is marked by offsetting slabs of rock that constrict the Chattooga to half-a-dozen yards. A white tongue protrudes into a deep hole that will spill a canoe if it enters at an angle. Roger and I made a clean run and bounded through the tail wave. The canyon walls closed in and the river deepened. I squatted low to keep my balance amid the swirls and boils. Beneath my paddle, specks of mica raced with the current.

A crescent of sand along the south-facing wall beckoned us to stop for lunch. We beached the canoes and unloaded our gear. The sandbar was perfect; not a footprint or wind drift marred its surface. We stretched out along its length, settled into its warmth.

Michael passed around a bag of gorp, a mixture of raisins, peanuts, and M&Ms that had been the staple of hikers and river runners since the health-conscious 1960s.

"Anyone care for a Honey Bun?" George asked.

Keith snarled. "Get that thing away from me."

George devoured the mitten-sized pastry, moaning with feigned delight.

"Now for the main course," he said. From his cooler, George brought out a prepackaged luncheon tray. He peeled back the plastic cover and pointed out the offerings. "Here you have your basic Ritz cracker with peanut butter. And over here, medallions of baloney. The dessert is some kind of mystery pudding. I just love that yellow dye."

"George, you are the anti-Christ," Michael said.

Now that we were on the river, I warmed up to Michael. He was utterly without pretense, full of enthusiasm and good humor. Roger, too, was in good spirits despite the morning's rocky start. He asked about my family, taking special interest in Jackson.

"I've got twin boys—four-year-olds," he said. "When Jackson gets a little older, we'll have to get them together."

"Are they much trouble?" I asked, remembering the twins that were once in my future.

Roger sighed. "The first few years were hell. Things are better now."

Karen gave a husky laugh. "Hell is right. I remember those nights you came over looking totally drained. All you wanted was to drink a beer and watch TV."

Karen seemed completely at ease in the company of men. She spoke up without hesitation and laughed as long and loud as the rest of us. She was a good canoeist, which gave her the standing to critique George and Michael's morning run. "You guys carved out a whole new route down Dick's Creek Ledge," she said. "They need to put that one in the guidebooks."

Michael laughed. "At least we made that turn."

"You sucked is what you did," Keith said.

Michael nodded in agreement. "We did suck."

I marveled at how Keith could do this—be brutally honest and somehow not offend his friends. I never criticized people to their faces—always behind their backs. I guessed Keith had been this way with them from the start. You either accepted him or you didn't.

We packed up the canoes and headed out of The Narrows. A break in the horizon marked the second of the big drops. Second Ledge mirrors Dick's Creek from above, but instead of falling in stages, it drops straight down. Seven feet.

"Are you up for running this?" I asked Roger.

"You go, John," he said without defense. "I'll take your picture to show to Cathy!"

Humbled once again, I put Roger off on the bank. Now that I was paddling solo, I changed positions in the canoe, kneeling just behind the center thwart to bring my weight and control closer to the midpoint. The boat spun easily as I pushed offshore, so much lighter with only one person. I approached the ledge and held my breath. The boat dropped through the air and landed with a hollow thud, upright, undamaged. Just like that, it was over. As my tripmates cheered, I thought of how much easier it would be to paddle solo all the time, maybe even buy one of those new short canoes. But that would have to wait.

Keith and Karen soared over the ledge, followed by Michael and George. The latter two looked good going over, but their combined

THE CANOEIST ➤ 146

weight did them in on impact. The Freighter nose-dived underwater, stalled and rolled. George surfaced and swam to the shallows, water dripping off his beard. "I'll have that film, Roger," he said.

With Second Ledge behind us, we paddled with growing confidence. Roger, too, seemed more at ease, his strokes quick and sure. We rode the big waves at the bottom of Rollercoaster, dashed through the squeeze at Eye of the Needle, and skirted the big rock at the bottom of Keyhole.

As the afternoon wore on, our energy faded. The sun shone in our faces, firing the surface with a blinding glare. Our paddling slowed; conversation dwindled. We were all thinking the same thing.

"We gonna run the Bull, Roger?" I asked.

"Not me. But you should do it."

"I don't know, man. I haven't decided."

A cluster of boats appeared on the western shore, their paddlers nowhere to be seen. We had arrived. We beached the canoes on the ledge and followed the well-trodden path to the rapid.

You hear Bull Sluice before you see it, a dull throb that vibrates the bedrock. Paddlers stand along the bluff, heads canted downward. A dozen feet below, the Chattooga boils inside a rock-rimmed cauldron, white and menacing. The cauldron is fed by a crystal sheet of water pouring over a five-foot ledge and spinning back on itself. This is where boaters flip. And sometimes drown. If you're lucky, the current pushes you out the cauldron and through a giant spigot—the "sluice."

Keith yelled, "I always think this isn't going to look as bad as I remembered it, but it's always worse."

"It'll tighten up your asshole," George said.

A canoe bobbed down the narrow channel and into the pool above the ledge. The pool is just big enough to circle your boat into an eddy along the shore, to slow your momentum and line yourself up for the right-angle drop into the cauldron. The canoeists started their turn, but a fraction too late. The stern swung in a slow arc just above the ledge. The current pulled the boat backward, and the paddlers tumbled over the ledge, bobbed to the surface and circled halfway around the bowl. They shot out the sluice and into the slow water below, shaken but unhurt.

"That's it," Karen said. "I'm walking."

Roger nodded. "Ditto for me."

My stomach pulled into a knot. I thought once again of Carrie McCune, how quickly a person could drown. But if I didn't run it this time, I never would.

"What do you say, Keith?"

Keith shrugged. "I'll run it if you will."

"Michael?"

Michael conferred with George. "We could possibly run this straight through if we stay to the inside. What do you think?"

"Beats trying to eddy out the Freighter."

Keith and I offered to stand by the ledge with throw ropes if George and Michael would run the rapid first. I hiked back to the canoe and grabbed the yellow nylon bag with the thirty-foot length of rope coiled inside. I hadn't ever practiced throwing this thing and hoped not to have to use it now.

Minutes passed before the Freighter came around the bend. George and Michael looked as grim as prisoners, eyes lifeless, faces slack. They hugged the inside of the channel and the pool beyond, but had no time to adjust to the oncoming ledge.

Keith frowned. "They're screwed."

The canoe landed at an angle and flipped. I readied the throw bag, but saw only the tops of my friends' red helmets rushing past beneath the foam. They reappeared in the clear spout, tucked in the fetal position. They splashed into the pool and crawled to the nearby shore.

"They're okay," I called to Keith.

The Freighter was not so lucky. Sucked sideways into the hydraulic at the base of the ledge, the canoe spun around twice and disappeared underwater. From deep within the bowels of the cauldron came the hollow thud of a plastic hull being kicked and gored. It remained out of sight for long seconds, then, to the exclamations of the crowd, erupted skyward like a breaching whale. It washed out the chute and drifted upside down, dented but in one piece.

Keith volunteered to go next. He was hardly gone five minutes before appearing at the head of the rapid. Keith does things by the book, so I was not surprised that he chose to eddy out above the ledge. He paused along the shore to catch his breath, then ferried back into midstream. Three, four, five strokes, he paddled against the current until he was centered above the ledge, then swung his boat around.

Keith's landing was perfect, but he hesitated to take a stroke and the canoe lost its forward momentum. The stern submerged under the sheet of falling water. He rolled and disappeared. I waited with the rope. Where the hell was he? Yards downstream a hand broke the surface, twisting and turning in the air. By the time he came up for a breath, Keith was on his way out the sluice.

"Goddamn Bull," he gasped as I helped him onto the bank. "I got spun around underwater and couldn't tell which way was up."

Now I was plenty scared. But I saw what had to be done. I walked back to the put-in, dizzy with fear.

Before taking the field for my high school soccer team, I would loosen up on the sidelines. "Get out there and light a fire, Manuel!" Coach Molten would yell. Alone at the put-in, I went through the same routine—taking deep breaths, running in place, shaking my arms loose. All these years later, I still had something to prove. To my father? To Shephard? They were all in there somewhere. But mostly I wanted to prove to myself that I had the courage to run Bull Sluice.

I settled into the canoe and pushed off. The swift current swept me along the narrow channel toward the pool at the head of the Sluice. As soon as the bow passed into slow water, I shoved my paddle in sideways and wrestled the canoe into the eddy. My friends waited downstream, only their heads visible above the ledge. They held their ropes in the air and waved me onward. I came out to meet the Bull.

An observer on the shore can easily recall a boater's progress through a rapid—the narrowly missed boulder, the canoe plunging through the waves, water streaming from the hull. For the paddler, it's all a blur—flashes of light and shadow, a rush of wind and noise. I don't remember a thing after coming out of the eddy. But I do remember riding the sluice, splitting the air with a rebel yell.

CHAPTER TEN

The Nantahala

Keith threw a log on the fire and settled into his lawn chair. Laughter rose and fell from the neighboring campsites along the Nantahala River. A bottle of Jack Daniels had already circled our campfire once, and George was getting loud.

"Hey, John, tell us about the time you nearly blew up your dad's garage!" he said.

I laughed. "You want to hear that one again?"

"Yeah, Dad, tell it," Jackson said. "I haven't heard this one."

Jackson leaned forward in his seat, grinning in anticipation. I felt a little uneasy talking in front of my ten-year-old son about my years as a minor delinquent. Cathy wouldn't approve, fearful that I would be setting a bad example. But George had opened the door, and refusing to say anything would just make Jackson more curious.

"When I was a kid, one of my weekly chores was to take the garbage out and burn it in this incinerator in our garage," I began. "This one summer had been really humid, and the paper wouldn't light. So I stuffed one bag in after another until Dad finally noticed and told me I had to burn it. I tried a couple of matches, but the paper still wouldn't light. So I looked around and saw this can of gasoline…"

Truth was I loved telling these stories to my friends, recounting the ways I'd pissed off my father by playing the fool. The stories were my way of blowing off my own anger, of not having to confront him with that difficult emotion. I didn't worry that Jackson might adopt the same behavior. We were as close as a father and son could be. We could talk about anything.

"So I poured some gas down this cardboard tube, first a little, then a lot. I threw in a match and ducked."

Jackson sat wide-eyed, his face aglow in the firelight.

"The incinerator exploded. The door flew off. There was burning garbage everywhere. Dad came running from the kitchen and threw his hands on top of his head. I jumped into the station wagon to back it out and Dad started screaming, 'Don't start the car! Don't start the car!' But I knew it was just burning paper. I backed both cars into the driveway and brushed the paper off with a broom. Nothing ended up being damaged."

George broke into a devilish grin. "So did your dad pound you?"

I shook my head. "No. He was just glad I wasn't hurt."

Michael whooped. Keith buried his face in his hands.

"Jackson, don't ever do that to your dad," Roger said. Jackson smiled and sipped his soda; the whiskey started around again.

For so long, I'd dreamed of introducing Jackson to the canoeing life, to the joys of camping and the company of men. George's son, Jacob, had canoed with us for almost five years before going off to college. Roger and Michael had brought their sons on several trips. No doubt Keith and Karen's four-year-old, Christopher, would join us one day.

By default we had become an all-male group. Since Christopher's birth, Karen had opted to pass on these whitewater trips. Cathy, too, preferred staying at home with our second child, Allison. I missed not having Cathy along, but she said she was happy for me to have a weekend with my friends and to bring Jackson into the fold. She had witnessed the estrangement between me and my father and didn't want it repeated.

Jackson pulled a burning stick from the fire and held it before his face. He was a good-looking kid—curly blond hair, fierce brow, green eyes. He seemed completely at ease in the company of adults, laughing at our jokes, throwing in his own one-liners recalled from TV shows and movies. Tomorrow, we'd find out what he could do on the river.

Jackson and I had started canoeing the year before on the Eno and the Upper Haw. He loved running the rapids, quickly mastering the basic strokes, but was impatient with the long stretches of flatwater. We moved on to the Lower Haw.

"That's more like it," he said after our successful first descent through Gabriel's Bend.

I had to remind myself that the water level was low—six inches on the Bynum gauge—and that I was doing most of the steering. Still, Jackson seemed to be a natural in the bow. He responded to my commands with quick, agile moves, leaning out to plant his paddle as if he'd been doing it for years. This kid was ready for the Nantahala.

I conferred with Cathy about taking Jackson along on what had become my annual spring trip with "the guys."

"Just be careful," she said. "He might not be as ready as you think."

"We'll be fine," I said.

I explained to Jackson that we would be driving up to the mountains, camping out at night and running the river during the day.

"The Nantahala's a great river," I said. "Lots of rapids. It's not dangerous, but there's a chance we could tip over, especially if we decide to run the Falls. The water's pretty cold."

Jackson seemed to contemplate that last statement. "Will we have enough to eat?"

In the darkness surrounding our campsite, a dozen fires glowed. Car doors slammed; televisions flickered through RV windows. This wasn't the backwoods camping experience I preferred, but it didn't seem to bother Jackson. On several of our camping trips to wilder haunts, he'd woken up constantly, imagining bears and burglars just outside the tent. This night he slept soundly.

In the morning, we piled into our cars and headed to the River's End Restaurant. The Nantahala Outdoor Center next door was not yet open, its parking lot virtually empty. Two decades earlier, the NOC had begun as a family-run rafting company operating out of a one-story cinder-block motel. Now, it was a burgeoning empire with two restaurants, boat rentals, international guided trips, and a retail/mail order business that generated more than $10 million in annual sales.

We settled into a table by the window so Jackson could enjoy a view of Nantahala Falls. The falls is the signature rapid on the Nantahala River, a boulder-lined narrows with a four-foot plunge at the end. On summer afternoons, as many as a hundred onlookers might gather along the road to watch the parade of boaters ride the roaring plume. But at this hour, the banks were empty and the falls a mere trickle.

Like many rivers in the Southern Appalachians, the flow of the Nantahala is controlled by a power company. The Tennessee Valley Authority built a dam and powerhouse at the head of the Nantahala Gorge in the 1930s, channeling the water impounded in the lake through turbines to produce electricity.

During World War II, the hydroplant sold most of its electricity to the Alcoa aluminum smelters in east Tennessee, which were building bombers to support the war effort. Later, the plant became part of a larger regional grid owned by Nantahala Power & Electric Co., providing power to homes and businesses during periods of peak electrical demand. In summer, that peak demand typically occurs on weekdays from late morning through early evening when air conditioners are running. The rest of the time, the floodgates are closed and the river runs dry.

As river running became more popular in the 1970s and '80s, citizens were able to pressure the power company to release water on weekends. Once that happened, the Nantahala became a playland for boaters of every variety—rafters, kayakers, and canoeists. As we ate our breakfast, fellow paddlers filled the restaurant until every seat was taken. It was going to be a busy day on the "Nanty."

We paid our bill and stepped outside to find the street clogged with traffic. School buses loaded with rafts overhead groaned around the curve, passengers hooting and waving out the windows. Veteran river runners, men and women with deep tans and sinewy bodies, strode past us with kayaks on their shoulders.

Back at camp, I hurried Jackson through his morning chores. "Get your paddling clothes on and brush your teeth," I said. "The river will be running in twenty minutes."

"Jeez, Dad, take it easy."

"And don't forget to go to the bathroom."

The parking lot at the put-in was jammed. Some guides stood atop the buses tossing rafts onto the pavement, while others gathered their clients in noisy clusters on the lawn. Dressed in his loose-fitting, quick-dry shirt and too-large helmet, Jackson looked impossibly small next to these college-aged students and adults. But I couldn't wait for them to see what he could do on the river. We would show these people how to paddle a canoe.

This was our inaugural run in my new canoe, a powder blue Dagger Caption. A mere fourteen feet long with a "rockered" hull (curved up at each end for easier turning), the Caption was one of the new breed of canoes specifically designed for whitewater. The boat was outfitted with a three-position foam saddle, allowing it to be paddled tandem or solo. And every square inch not needed for seating was taken up by air bags designed to keep the boat riding high in the event of a capsize.

Still wedded to the straight lines and traditional red or green colors of the classic canoes, I had been slow to warm to these new boats with their banana-shaped hulls in purple, mango, and orange. The

Caption was the least offensive of the lot. And having tested one on the Nantahala the year before, I knew how it could perform, responding to every stroke, bobbing over waves like a cork.

We carried the boats across the parking lot and took our place in line for the put-in, a garage-sized boat basin dug into the side of the Nantahala.

Jackson frowned. "How come there aren't more canoes?"

I surveyed the assortment of watercraft—kayaks, rafts, and "duckies," a one-person inflatable kayak. Ours were the only canoes.

"Rafts are better for people who don't have a lot of experience," I said. "They're real stable, and they bounce off rocks. I don't like them 'cause they're hard to steer and slow on flatwater."

I confessed I didn't know too much about duckies, but it looked like the paddler was frequently getting wet.

"How about kayaks?" he asked.

"Kayaks are cool. They're more maneuverable than canoes, but you have to learn to roll 'em, which I've never done. Besides, I like paddling with other people."

I didn't tell Jackson, and hated to admit it to myself, but canoes, even the newer models, were becoming scarce on whitewater rivers. Younger paddlers were all going to kayaks and duckies. Canoes were too stodgy for this generation.

We slid the Caption into the calm waters of the boat basin. I tightened the straps around my thighs and blew some extra air into the flotation bag. Keith and Roger set the yellow canoe in behind us, followed by George and Michael in the Freighter.

Beyond the boat basin, the Nantahala rushed past, gin-clear water tumbling over a bed of small rocks. As we paddled into the current, the Dagger yawed upstream. Jackson grabbed the gunwales.

"Don't do that!" I said.

"We were about to tip over, Dad!"

"No, we weren't. This boat feels tippier than the Mad River, but it's not about to roll."

I tried to explain the concept of secondary stability, how these whitewater canoes were designed to tilt on edge for easier turning and surfing, but not to roll beyond a certain point. Jackson was skeptical.

"Let's just try and go straight," he said.

We turned downstream, caught up in a sea of moving boats. Raft guides jockeyed for position, exhorting their crews to paddle. Kayakers darted in between; a duckie spun backward. I'd seen crowds on the Nantahala before, but this was ridiculous.

Around the first bend lay Patton's Run, a rapid characterized by a large, barely submerged boulder right in the middle of the river. I instructed Jackson to stay to the left and brace through the wave.

We rounded the bend to find a canoe broached on the rock, its bow sticking right in our path.

"Draw right!"

Jackson pulled hard, the sinew flexing in his thin arms. We slipped through the narrow gap between the rock and the shore, punched through the tail wave, and eddied out against the bank.

"Good job!" I said.

Keith and Roger came around the corner, dodged the canoe, and swung in behind us.

THE NANTAHALA

"We would've hit that boat if we hadn't seen you boogey for shore," Roger said. "Way to go, Jackson."

Keith nodded his approval. I felt a sudden wave of emotion and glanced away to hide my tears. I couldn't understand what was happening. Was it just Jackson I was happy for, or was there another boy in the boat who'd waited a lifetime for a few words of praise?

Beyond Patton's Run, the river descended between outstretched branches of hemlock and rhododendron. The water shone ice blue, reflecting the wedge of clear sky between the high mountains.

"Nantahala," the Cherokees call it, "Land of the Noonday Sun." So steep and tall are the surrounding ridges that parts of the gorge never see direct sunlight in winter. Even in summer, long stretches of river lie in shadow as early as 2 PM. And the water is cold—forty-five degrees where it emerges from beneath the dam just upstream of the put-in. When the air is humid, a mist settles over the river, sometimes in the morning, sometimes the still of the evening, a gauze so thick you can hardly see the sky. Today we had a clear view, leaving nothing to fear as long as we stayed out of the water.

We raced beneath the Highway 19 bridge and skirted the big wave beside Delebar's Rock. I admired how the Caption handled, its upturned nose rising with the waves instead of plowing through them as my old canoe did. By canting my hips, I could tilt the boat to one side or the other to deflect spray or lean into a turn. There was more yet to learn from this new style of canoeing.

The current on the Nantahala never stops, and in our featherlight canoe, I felt as if we were flying. We overtook pods of rafts and duckies, their crews looking on with a mixture of admiration and jealousy.

"I wish I had me one of them canoes," a man called out, reminding me again how much I loved this craft, ancient or modern.

Jackson paddled with confidence, switching sides, reaching out on his draws. I caught an occasional glimpse of his face in profile—serious, proud—as we passed a boat or a bystander on the bank.

I glanced over my shoulder to find that our friends had fallen far behind. We pulled into an eddy and waited. Keith and Roger were the first to arrive.

"You need to slow down," Keith admonished. "For a while I couldn't even see you guys."

I had forgotten one of the fundamental rules of canoeing—always keep your partners in sight. Things can go wrong quickly on a river. One moment you're upright, the next you're pinned on a rock. If your partners have gone around the bend, they will be unable to help. Jackson and I were on top of the world now, but the situation could easily happen where we needed to be rescued.

George and Michael pulled up in the Freighter. "You feeling hungry, boy?" George grinned to Jackson. "Q Shack is right around the corner."

Six miles below the put-in, the Nantahala passes a barbecue shack built right on the banks of the river. I had always turned my nose up at the notion of stopping for takeout in the middle of a run. Jackson had no such reservations.

"Do they have milkshakes?" he asked.

"Sure they do," George said. Seeing my frown, he added. "Better check with your dad."

After a half-hour break at the Q shack, we headed back on the

Nantahala. A railroad track paralleled the river on the north bank. Above the rush of water, I heard a distinct huffing.

Steam locomotives had disappeared from the rails when I was a toddler, but the memory of those fantastic machines lingered on. I knew better than to hope that I would see one out here in the midst of a whitewater run. The huffing grew louder.

"Holy shit, Jackson, look at this!"

Around the bend came a giant steam engine, wreathed in a plume of gray smoke. Pistons flying, drive wheels spinning, the locomotive pulled a line of coaches bearing the moniker of the Great Smoky Mountains Railway. Passengers leaned through the open windows, waving at the man and boy in the powder blue canoe. I threw down my paddle and waved back.

"Dad!" Jackson yelled. "Keep hold of your paddle."

Baffled by my son's lack of interest, I watched the engine disappear around the bend, its pulsating breath soon overlapped by the rush of the rapids.

In the seventh mile, the river begins its winding descent toward Nantahala Falls. I hadn't decided yet whether or not Jackson and I would run the falls. We were having a great run, but this rapid was considerably more difficult than anything we'd encountered upstream. I spotted the path used to scout the rapid and pulled ashore.

George stepped out of the Freighter and wrapped Jackson in a burly arm. "My butthole always acts up when I get to this point," he grimaced. "How 'bout you? Feelin' a little runny?"

I loved the way George behaved with Jackson. He was the funny uncle, the guy who could get away with saying anything. No matter how outrageous his humor, there was always a measure of sympathy. Jackson grinned as we headed down the trail.

Cars lined the shoulder of the road paralleling the river to the south. Above the rush of falling water, I could hear the cheers of the crowd as boaters dropped over the falls. We arrived to find the wooden viewing stand packed with bystanders, cameras and camcorders held high. I found an opening along the guardrail and pulled Jackson in beside me.

Nantahala Falls is more like a pour-over than falls — a ten-yard-wide plunge over a sloping rock ledge. But the approach is tricky. A hole on "river right" — the right side of the river facing downstream — can snag unsuspecting boaters. The hole can be avoided by hugging the inside of the bend, but that puts paddlers above the steepest part of the falls and in front of a standing wave that will flip canoes and kayaks entering at an angle.

I pointed out the best route to Jackson. "We want to stay to the left of that hole. As soon as we pass it, draw the bow toward the right. I'll try to line us up going over the falls. When we hit that wave, paddle like hell."

We watched a trio of kayakers surf the wave below the falls, doing enders and three-sixties. A pod of rafts ploughed through, crew cheering as they bounced over the drop.

"Whaddya say, Jackson?"

"Let's watch a few more."

Just as we were about to leave, a group of boys paddling a small raft drifted into the hole above the falls. The raft momentarily stalled, disgorging one of its passengers out the back. While his buddies paddled blithely onward, the boy spun in the hole, eyes and mouth forming circles of mute alarm.

A wet-suited figure leapt into the pool and grabbed the boy by his life jacket. With a few swift kicks, the man brought him safely ashore. The crowd clapped, and the parade of rafts resumed.

Jackson frowned. "I don't know about this, Dad."

"Don't worry," I said. "I can get us past that hole."

Nantahala Falls is not a killer. Since the 1970s when commercial rafting began, tens of thousands of people have run this rapid and only a handful have drowned. But I figured Jackson and I had a fifty-fifty chance of flipping going over the falls. If he went in that frigid water, maybe banged his shins, Jackson would be shocked. His feelings about canoeing might change, and not just for this trip. I'd seen how he reacted on the soccer field, swooning in the face of minor scrapes and bruises. I had to keep that boat upright.

"You guys gonna do it?" Keith asked.

I glanced at Jackson. "Yeah, we're going."

"I'll get my throw bag."

Once more in the boat, I went over the route with Jackson. "And when we hit that wave at the bottom…"

"I know. Paddle like hell."

Jackson hated swear words. It pained him to use one even in imitation of his father. I gave him a hug and settled into the stern. "Which side do you want?"

"Right. I already told you," he said.

"Okay. Let's do it."

We pushed off and rode the swift water around the bend. The current pulled us faster than I wanted. Was that the hole we just passed? Helmeted heads of kayakers loomed above a break in the waterline.

"Draw left," I shouted.

We plunged over the falls and hit the wave at an angle. The canoe jerked sideways, pitching Jackson halfway over the gunwale. I countered with a low brace, paddle pressed flat against the surface. For three long heartbeats, we hung in balance, the hull canted at a forty-five-degree angle. Then, as if a hand reached up from underneath, we rocked back to level.

A cheer went up from the crowd. Jackson shot his fist in the air. As a good canoeist must do, I put the moment of fear behind me. *We made it,* I told myself. *That's all that matters for now.*

CHAPTER ELEVEN

The Pigeon

For as long as I have lived in North Carolina, I have harbored a dream: somewhere in the wooded folds of the Appalachians, a river lies undiscovered. It's a small river, hissing over beveled ledges, hidden from view by hemlock and rhododendron. The locals know about it, the cane pole fishermen and the farmers. But not the kayakers and canoeists hailing from far-off urban sprawls.

I will discover the river and introduce it to a select group of friends. Together, we will explore the winding channel, ascribe names to the rapids, and revel in sun-dappled pools. My friends will marvel that I could find such a place, and we will promise to keep it a secret.

Fifteen years after I moved to the South, this dream almost came true.

The year before we married, Cathy and I drove to meet her parents at their family farm in Knoxville, Tennessee. A visit to the Murphy farm was a trip back in time. The Murphy ancestors had settled the land around 1800; the farmhouse we slept in was at least a century old. Most days, we would sit outside with Cathy's parents and her Tennessee relatives talking about the weather and who was taking care of the cows. But my thoughts kept drifting back to the river I'd glimpsed on the ride over.

Between Canton, North Carolina, and Newport, Tennessee, Interstate 40 follows a winding gorge through the heart of the southern Appalachian Mountains. There's a river at the bottom of that gorge, though most of the time it lies hidden beneath a thick canopy of trees.

As Cathy and I drove west that summer day, I craned my neck to see past the guardrail. Finally, a bridge loomed ahead. I lowered my window and whiffed the sulfurous odor of rotten eggs. The mountains parted to reveal a dark ribbon of water streaked with white.

"Look at those rapids!" I blurted. "Check that sign and tell me the name of the river."

As we came off the bridge, Cathy peered across the interstate. "Pigeon River," she said. "That's an odd name."

The Pigeon. I seemed to remember reading something about that river in the newspaper, and it wasn't good. As we passed out of the mountains into the Tennessee foothills, a billboard appeared beside the highway: "Pigeon River Just Ahead, Polluted by Champion International. Lord Help Us, EPA Won't."

Back in Durham, I asked Howard DuBose at River Runner's Emporium about the Pigeon. He came out from behind the counter into the crowded confines of his shop. "Damn right, it's polluted," Howard said. "Gets sucked into Champion's paper mill in Canton and comes out black as tar. Stinks, too. North Carolina refuses to crack down on the mill because they don't want to lose the jobs, so Tennessee's trying to get the EPA to step in. But the feds won't enforce their own damn law."

I asked how long the river had been polluted.

"Since 1908," Howard said. "The year they opened the mill."

I laughed at the irony. 1908 was the year my father had been born.

"What about the rapids?" I asked. "Looked like some nice ones."

"Supposed to be Class III and IVs, but no one wants to go near the water. Besides, C.P.&L. has a hydro plant at the top of the gorge that cuts off the flow when they aren't making electricity. They refuse to tell the public when it's going to run. Who wants to drive five hours to find the river dry?"

Howard's message all but killed my hopes for the Pigeon. Yet each summer when Cathy and I traveled to Knoxville, I found myself stealing glances through the trees.

Then, a break. Under pressure from the State of Tennessee and a citizen's group called the Dead Pigeon River Council, the Environmental Protection Agency agreed to step in and impose stiffer requirements on the North Carolina mill. The agency ordered Champion to lighten its wastewater discharge to meet a monthly average of fifty color units—roughly the color of ginger ale. And Champion promised to install water recycling equipment to try to reduce the smell. Champion announced a half-billion dollars in plant improvements to be started within the year.

Meanwhile, the power company's license for the hydroelectric plant on the Pigeon came up for renewal. A new federal law required that recreational interests be considered along with power generation needs as a condition for awarding a license. Rafting outfitters in Tennessee demanded regularly scheduled releases of water, similar to what was practiced on the Nantahala.

That winter, I called a state environmental officer in Tennessee and learned that Champion had already brought some of its new systems on line. The color of the effluent was lightening and the odor was down. "But, no, nobody's running the river that I know of. Some reputations die hard," he said.

I began to see my dream taking shape, not the remote pristine river that I'd imagined, but a passable variation. There would be a period of time, maybe a year or two, when the Pigeon was clean enough to run, but not yet recognized as such by the boating public. I could be the one to rediscover the river, or, rather, my friends and I.

That spring, I argued for taking our annual canoe trip to the Pigeon. Keith hesitated on the phone.

"Why would we want to run a polluted river?" he asked.

"I'm telling you, man, it's getting better. And what's a little odor for the chance to discover someplace new?"

"Your standards must be a lot different from mine," he said. "Then again, you grew up paddling the Cuyahoga."

We ended up that year canoeing the French Broad, northern neighbor to the Pigeon and none too clean in its own right. The following winter, I learned that an outfitter named Jerry Taylor had moved to the riverside town of Hartford, Tennessee, in anticipation of starting a commercial rafting business on the Pigeon. I phoned Jerry and introduced myself. Would he be willing to guide me and a group of friends down the Pigeon in May?

"Sure thing, dude," Jerry said. "Y'all can stay with me."

✢

Hartford, Tennessee, was one of those towns that interstate drivers blow past without a second glance. No billboards heralded its coming. The mountains opened only briefly for the lone exit. The Exxon station closed at 9 PM. The general store, which doubled as a post office, lacked even a lighted sign.

Jerry lived in a ramshackle house beneath the hacked-off face of a mountain. Keith navigated the van and canoe trailer up the eroded driveway and parked next to a rusting school bus. Jerry sat in a rocker on the front porch, bushy-haired and shirtless. I guessed him to be in his early thirties.

"Is this okay?" George called out the window as the van settled into a pothole.

"Suits me," Jerry said.

"I wasn't sure if it was assigned parking."

Jerry caught the glint in George's eye and ventured a slow smile. "I'd invite y'all inside, but there ain't nothin' in the way of furniture. You'll probably want to pitch your tents out back."

We followed Jerry around the house to a narrow wedge of lawn. There was just enough room for three tents.

"Mind if we build a fire?" Keith asked.

"No problem," Jerry said. "Just pull some of them rocks out of the garden and make you a fire ring."

"On the lawn?"

Jerry shrugged. "I'm just rentin'."

We set up camp and built a fire with branches snapped from a dying dogwood. Keith produced one of his signature meals—blackened chicken with wild rice and asparagus. Michael brought out the plastic wine glasses and uncorked a bottle of Chardonnay.

"Damn, you guys know how to eat!" Jerry said.

After the Jack Daniels had gone around the circle, I asked Jerry to tell us about the Pigeon.

"It's a kick-ass river," he said. "Seven Class IIIs and one Class IV. 'Course, it depends whether C.P.&L.'s generating or not. The feds are supposed to issue that license for the Walters Plant some time this year. If they give us scheduled releases at least five days a week, this place'll be hoppin'."

"Anything in the water to worry about?" Roger asked.

"Not unless you plan on drinkin' it," Jerry said.

Michael opened a tin of chocolate chip cookies and passed it around the circle. "What's the plan for tomorrow?" he asked.

"River should be crankin' up about 10 AM. C.P.&L.'s been running Walters at about forty megawatts—a little low for my taste—but it'll make some waves."

"What are we talking about, one- to two-footers?" Roger asked.

"Hell, you say. Three- to four-footers at least."

Keith laughed. "You need to understand who you're dealing with, Jerry. Three-foot waves are more than enough to sink this crowd."

"You hard boaters," Jerry sniffed. "You need to get in some duckies. They'll ride right over that shit. Got a couple extra if anyone wants to try."

Michael sat up. "I might be interested in that."

Michael asked George if he would mind paddling the Freighter alone.

"Anything we can do to lighten the load," George said.

In truth, we were all coming to realize that paddling solo was the best way to tackle pushy rivers. Tandem boats were too hard to maneuver and took on too much water. Keith and Roger had purchased solo boats shortly after I bought the Caption. Keith had urged George and Michael to do the same.

In the morning, Jerry pulled two deflated duckies out of his stack of five. "I'm pretty sure these'll hold air," he said.

He plugged in his electric pump, strolled over to the school bus, and opened the back door. "Stick your boats in here. We'll leave your van in town."

"You're going to use the *bus* to carry five of us to the put-in?" Keith asked.

"Sure, dude. Gotta keep it tuned for my customers."

As the rest of us piled into the mold-scented bus, George jogged to the van and dug in the glove compartment. He came back with a small floating compass attached to a suction cup.

"I've been looking for somewhere to put this," he said. He pushed the compass onto the hood of the bus and flashed his devilish grin.

Jerry cranked the engine and we rumbled up the interstate, George hollering at every turn. "Which way are we headed now, Jerry?"

We exited the interstate at the North Carolina/Tennessee line, wound down a crumbling two-lane highway and across a cement bridge. The Pigeon rolled out from underneath, solid whitewater in both directions.

I turned to Keith with a smug grin. "See, man? What did I tell you?"

"As long as I don't die from dioxin poisoning," he answered.

The put-in lay in the shadow of the Walters Plant, a handsome turn-of-the-century brick building with tall windows and decorative molding at the corners. Three cavernous arches penetrated the foundation, from which emerged a dark, sulfurous brew.

"Whoo, boy," George said. "I'll need to wash my clothes tonight."

"You'll get used to it," Jerry said. "Couple miles down, you won't smell a thing."

We slid our boats down the steep bank and started loading the gear. Before anyone else had his life jacket on, Jerry was in his duckie, surfing the waves below the power plant.

Michael looked befuddled. "Hey, Jerry, Aren't you gonna tell me how to paddle this thing?"

"Get in it and go," Jerry yelled. "Best way to learn."

With that, our guide headed off, swept up like a leaf in the wind. I climbed in my canoe, almost flipped as I pushed off shore, and turned downstream.

The rapid below the powerhouse ran nonstop for a quarter of a mile. Watery plumes kicked up by subsurface rocks sprouted all across the surface. Cross-currents buffeted my canoe. I caught up to Jerry and eddied out behind a huge boulder.

"Hold on, man," I said. "I've got a boat full of water."

Jerry shook his head and pointed to Michael bobbing over the waves in his duckie. "See what I mean? Duckies rule."

"Oh, yeah? I'll be sure to wait for you when we hit the flat water."

"Ain't no flat water on this sucker," Jerry said.

As we waited for the others to arrive, I gazed at the elephantine boulder sitting curiously in midstream. It was ten times the size of anything else in the river. "How do you think this thing got here?" I asked.

"Must've rolled down the mountain when they were blasting for I-40," he said. "Ain't nothing gonna move this thing."

I had worried that our trip would be marred by the presence of the interstate running just a few hundred feet above us. But the steep, wooded bank hid the view of the road, and the rush of water masked the sound of the passing vehicles. For all we would see or hear, we might as well be in a wilderness.

After a quick bailing of the canoes, we headed on downstream. The current swept us under the Waterville Road bridge and into a narrow gorge. Every bend threw up another Class III rapid, another series of obstacles to be deciphered on the run. It was the kind of canoeing I loved.

Appalachian Mountain rivers rarely offer a distant view, and the Pigeon was no exception. But in the second mile, the river straightened out, descending a long, white staircase to the base of a camel-backed mountain. I pulled over to take a picture and watched our procession of boats angle from one side to the next, sliding and leveling, sliding and leveling.

At the bottom of the run, the hills closed in again. The current piled against one bank, a long wave train disappearing around the bend. Jerry circled into an eddy and, for the first time, offered us instructions.

"This one's a Class IV," Jerry said. "Ride that wave train until you get to that boulder on the right-hand bank, then hang a sharp left."

Roger peered downriver. "This doesn't look bad. What makes it a IV?"

Jerry smiled. "You'll see."

Bending his long torso over his outstretched knees, Jerry propelled his duckie downstream.

"Give us a signal when you get to the bottom," Keith called.

Jerry dropped from view, his whirling kayak paddle the last thing I saw. We waited for him to reappear on the bank. Minutes passed.

"You think he's planning to wave us on?" Keith asked.

Michael laughed. "Who, Jerry?"

My nerves started buzzing. "Hell, I'm going," I said. "I'll signal you guys when I get through."

I set off along the right-hand bank, just out of reach of the fluttering alders. The bow pitched up and down with the rising waves. Then, as if a door had opened onto some enormous engine room, the sound of the river changed. An ominous roar filled the air; the water turned white from bank to bank. I plunged into a maelstrom of holes and cross-currents, struggled to keep my balance. There was Jerry in the middle of the rapid, aimed upstream, riding an enormous wave. I flew past, glided into an aerated pool, and pulled out on shore, stunned.

The bluff along the bank offered a view back upstream. I scaled its craggy face and signaled the others on with a wave of my paddle. One by one, they worked their way through, arriving breathless at the bottom of the rapid. Jerry, meanwhile, was turning three-sixties in the middle of the river, happy as a seal.

George shook his head. "Guys, we're in the presence of either greatness or lunacy. I'm not sure which."

Tired of waiting for our guide, I led the way downstream. The Pigeon slowed as it backed up behind a vein of rock protruding from the bank. I stood in my canoe, saw how the channel narrowed into a dark tongue that dropped briefly out of sight and into a quiet pool beyond. The rapid looked harmless, so I proceeded onward. I slid down the tongue and up the crest of the first wave. The hole on the far side took me by surprise. My stomach dropped as the canoe swooped down and up again, teetered on the crest of the second wave, and rolled over sideways.

I made it to shore with a few swift kicks, dragging my canoe behind me. I stood on the gravel bar and waved my arms. "Watch out for the hole!" I shouted. "It's a big one."

Keith came first, eyes wide, frozen in mid-stroke. He swooped down and up the waves, his face resolving to a smile as he glided safely into the pool. "Man, that was awesome! I want to do that one again."

We watched as the others rode the rapid, each one grinning as they came ashore. We pulled the boats over the gravel bar and ran the rapid a second time. Jerry went back for thirds.

Wet and exhausted, we decided to break for lunch. I set my soda in the river to cool and noted the color of the water. It looked about like iced tea, not much different from the rivers in eastern North Carolina with their natural load of tannins. But the local activists wanted further improvements. Jerry said the Dead Pigeon River Council was demanding that Champion lighten its effluent to match that of other mountain rivers. And its members weren't happy that he was promoting the Pigeon as ready for recreation.

I leaned back on my elbows, stared at the sun-dappled river and the hemlocks on the far shore. We could stay here all day and never see another person. This was it. This was my dream.

"Say, Jerry, has anybody named these rapids?" I asked.

"Somebody named the IIIs and IVs a few years back. This one's called Roostertail."

I sniffed. "Roostertail. That's kind of anticlimactic. Are these names published anywhere?"

"Not that I know of."

"So you could print your own map? Call 'em anything you want?"

Jerry shrugged. "I suppose. I've been meaning to print up a map for my customers."

I glanced around. "Whaddya think, guys? What's a better name for this rapid?"

George stroked his goatee. "How about Big Fucking Hole?"

Jerry shook his head. "Come on, dude, I can't print that on a map."

"Okay, then, BFH," George said.

Jerry nodded. "That'll work."

We broke into laughter. BFH. But this was how rapids got their names — Harold's Tombstone, Volkswagen Rock. They were all named at the whims of paddlers like us. Years from now, people would ask what BFH meant and where it came from. Guides would tell them, "Some guys from Durham and Chapel Hill. George Small, John Manuel…"

Late in the afternoon, we arrived at the take-out in Hartford. We loaded the canoes on the trailer and strolled over to the general store. The old woman behind the counter frowned with disapproval as we came through the door. I examined the selection of white bread, Spam, and Vienna sausages. "Dare I ask for a cappuccino?" George said.

Back outside, I took a bite of my stale candy bar and stared at the boarded-up schoolhouse. "This is where it's all going to happen," I said to George. "Outfitters' stores, parking lots…"

"How long do you think we have?" he asked.

"I figure another year, maybe two. Then people will find out what a great river this is. If Jerry plays his cards right, he'll make a killing."

George laughed. "Maybe. But I'm not sure Jerry's cut out for customer service."

⊸⊳

We came back to the Pigeon the following spring. Jerry had bought the general store and was doing double duty as checkout clerk and guide for the Smoky Mountain River Company. The water quality of the Pigeon was steadily improving, and C.P.&L. had agreed to start regularly scheduled water releases the following year. Fortunately for us, the masses had yet to discover the river.

"Let me ring these people up, and we'll get paddling," Jerry said. "Anybody know how to change the ribbon on this cash register?"

We waited in the parking lot while Jerry attended to his customers. George noticed that the compass was gone from the hood of Jerry's bus. He sighed. "Some things just aren't meant to last."

Back on the river, Jerry was a happy man. He flew down Powerhouse, the long rapid below the Walters Plant. He surfed the wave in the middle of Lost Guide and, just for fun, rode backward through

BFH. As we paused for lunch on the gravel bar, I marveled that we still had the Pigeon—and Jerry—to ourselves.

"Another year and you're going to be booked solid with paying customers," I said. "You won't have time for us."

Jerry shook his head. "Nah, I'll always take time off for you guys."

"Hey, what happened to the map?" Roger asked. "Did you ever print one up?"

"Just a hand-drawn thing, but I'm making photocopies," Jerry said. "It's got your rapid on it—BFH. Folks around here are already calling it that."

George slapped Jerry on the back. "You're a good man, Jerry. Just for that, I'm going to give you one of my baloney medallions."

"Dude, I'm honored."

⊷

When I called the store the following spring, a woman answered the phone. I asked for Jerry. She hesitated.

"Are you a friend?" she asked.

I said I was.

"I'm sorry to tell you this, but Jerry's passed on."

"He's dead?"

"Yes, sir. He was riding a horse across Big Creek. It had been raining a lot and the horse must have slipped off the bridge. They found him on the rocks."

⊷

It was another two years before I could muster the will to return to the Pigeon. Cathy, Jackson, Allison and I were in Knoxville for the annual family reunion. The kids were eager for adventure. I suggested a raft trip down the Pigeon.

Hartford had been transformed just as I'd imagined. Billboards lined the interstate, beckoning the public to raft the Pigeon. Outfitters had taken over the abandoned school house. A giant cinder-block boat barn claimed the empty lot by the river.

Our trip with Wildwater Adventures was scheduled for 3 PM, but the girl behind the counter informed us that the one o'clock group had become stuck in traffic and was running an hour late. She urged us to look around the gift shop.

I thumbed through the postcards and calendars. I asked the clerk if she had any maps of the Pigeon.

"No, but there's a T-shirt's got the names of the rapids on it," she said.

She sorted through the rack. "Here it is."

I held the shirt up to the light. Powerhouse, Lost Guide, Rooster-tail…

"What happened to BFH?" I asked. "Isn't there a rapid called BFH?"

The girl blanched at my sudden display of emotion. "Not that I know of."

I stomped outside and stared in the direction of the general store. Had Jerry never printed up the map? Was his word not taken as gospel? I returned to the girl at the counter.

"Did you know Jerry Taylor?" I asked.

"No, but I heard of him. They put a memorial plaque for him on Big Rock."

"The one below Powerhouse?"

She nodded. "You'll go right by it."

The school bus carrying the one o'clock trip arrived. Our group of twenty was ushered out back to the "briefing area," where Mike, our strapping young guide, lectured us on rafting safety.

"Don't put your foot under the center seat or someone could fall against your knee and break your leg," he instructed. "Don't let go of your paddle handle or you're likely to knock someone's teeth out. And if you fall out of the raft, don't ever try to stand up in the river. You could get your foot trapped under a rock and drown."

Allison wrapped her pale, thin arms around mine. "Dad, I'm not sure I want to do this."

"Don't worry, honey," I assured her. "You'll have a blast."

From a dripping pile left by the previous group, we picked out helmets, paddles, and life jackets. We boarded the bus and crowded into the seats. I stared at the pasty-faced clients with their chubby legs and soft hands. What the hell was I doing here?

At the put-in, we took our place in line behind half-a-dozen other rafts. Mike announced our seating assignments. "Mom, you take the middle right," he said to Cathy. "Dad, you're back next to me."

We carried the boat to the river and climbed aboard. Mike gave out last-minute paddling instructions: "When I say forward left, everybody on the left-hand side paddles forward," he said. "When I say back right, everybody on the right-hand side paddles backward. Got that?"

"Yes."

"I can't hear you."

"Yes!"

We pushed off the bank and drifted into Powerhouse. The air vibrated with a familiar roar. I braced myself for the cross-currents that had buffeted my canoe, but I felt nothing. The big raft plowed over the waves as smooth as a hearse.

Allison glanced back with a relieved grin. "That wasn't so bad, Daddy," she said.

"Good, honey. I'm glad."

The current slowed. I turned to Mike. "What does the Dead Pigeon River Council say about the river these days?" I asked.

"Who?"

"The Dead Pigeon River Council."

Mike had not heard of them.

"So what do *you* think about the water quality?" I asked.

Mike looked perplexed. "I don't know. Seems okay to me."

Big Rock loomed ahead. Near the top, a bronze rectangle flashed in the sun.

"There's Jerry's plaque!" I said. "Can we stop and take a look?"

I stabbed my paddle into the river, trying to slow the lumbering raft. But Mike had no time for dreams or reminiscence. He stared straight ahead, eager to keep on schedule. Cathy flashed me a pained look as I slumped in defeat.

"Full speed ahead!" shouted the pudgy kid in the bow, and in a moment we'd gone past.

CHAPTER TWELVE

The Chattooga Revisited

The rain started around midnight, a scattering of thumps on the tent fly that soon multiplied to a steady downpour. I listened to Jackson's breathing in the sleeping bag next to mine. At least *he* could sleep.

Somewhere down in the valley, the Chattooga was rising. At two feet on the Highway 76 gauge, a big hole would start to form on the rapid above Sandy Ford. At two and a half feet, the Narrows would wash out. And above that level, I had no idea how wild and malevolent the river might be.

Section III of the Chattooga was the logical next step for Jackson and me after running the Nantahala. I figured we could make it down everything except Bull Sluice, and that rapid we could walk around. This was assuming the river was at a level similar to what we'd encountered on past trips—a foot and a half to two feet. The gauge reading posted on the Internet had said it was right at the latter when we left Durham. The Weather Channel predicted only a slight chance of rain, so I felt confident we'd be all right. But now, of course, the rain had come.

I knelt inside my down cocoon and prayed. Should I cancel the trip? How could I know whether I was leading my son into grand adventure or disaster? I was answered only by the steady thrum of wind and rain.

At first light, I donned my rain jacket and pants and stepped outside the tent. The Georgia woods lay shrouded in fog. The kitchen tarp sagged under its load of rainwater. Without thinking, I pulled down on the edge of it and caught a blast of cold water in the face.

Keith emerged from his tent and rummaged through the cooking gear for the coffeepot.

"So what're you thinking about the river?" he asked.

"Don't know. Thought I'd go down to the bridge and check the gauge. Want to come?"

"No, thanks. I'll get breakfast going."

I drove out to the paved road and clicked on the radio. The weatherman was calling for clearing skies and temperatures in the low seventies. Good news.

At the bottom of the hill, I pulled onto the shoulder and stared at the water swirling beneath the bridge. Definitely high. I decided that if the gauge reading was three feet or above, Jackson and I weren't going. I slipped down the muddy trail and found the white metal bar poking out of the water. It read two feet eleven inches.

The rest of the crew was up by the time I returned—Michael,

Roger, and two new "members," Charlie and Randy Humble. Charlie was a friend from Chapel Hill who'd joined us on several trips down the Haw. A strapping forty-five-year-old with a slight paunch and a receding hairline, Charlie fit the age and temperament of our group. He was quick with a joke and glad to help out around camp. His brother, Randy, seemed a bit standoffish, but this was our first meeting. A lawyer from Knoxville in his mid-fifties, he eyed our group with a flinty gaze and a slow smile, his six-foot-two-inch frame leaning against his new SUV. Having grown up in east Tennessee and canoed the likes of the Nolichucky and the Ocoee, both Randy and Charlie were first-rate paddlers. Section III of the Chattooga would be a cakewalk for them.

I relayed the news about the river level to the group. "Sounds exciting," Charlie said. "Is that too high for you and Jackson?"

"I don't know. I've never done it at three feet."

Charlie nodded at his brother. "Randy will be paddling his kayak. He can always bail you out if you get into trouble."

I asked Keith what he thought.

"It's supposed to be a nice day," he said. "I'd hate to spend it sitting around camp."

Michael voiced his desire to paddle. Roger was silent.

I missed not having George along. In recent years, cartilage between two of his vertebrae had been breaking down to the point where he could no longer paddle. I begged him to come to the Chattooga, but he was adamant in his refusal. If he were here now, he'd say something to lighten the mood.

I weighed our options. Jackson and I could sit around camp all day and wait for the others to return, then drive five hours back to Durham, or we could trust that we'd make it down the river with a little help from our friends. I roused Jackson and explained the situation.

"Whatever you think is best," he said.

I took a deep breath. "Okay. Let's do it."

With the promise of a sunny day, I urged Jackson to wear only his quick-dry shorts and shirt under his rain jacket and pants. But as we stepped out of the van at the trailhead to Earl's Ford, a chilly wind blew beneath an unbroken raft of gray clouds. We lowered the boats from the trailer and started dragging them downhill.

"How far to the river?" Jackson asked.

"About half a mile."

"Half a mile!"

"What are you complaining about? I'm the one pulling the boat."

We finally reached the clearing by the river, the muscles in my lower back and arms locked tight and burning. The silent, swirling waters at the put-in offered little portent of what was to come.

"This doesn't look too bad," Jackson said.

I nodded. "It gets tougher farther down."

As the rest of us loaded the canoes, Randy jumped into his kayak, paddled out to midstream, and practiced rolling. I sensed that Randy wasn't much aware of or concerned with our limitations as canoe-ists—or as individuals—but I trusted he'd help out if any of us got into trouble.

I put the Caption in the water and settled in the rear saddle. As Jackson lowered himself in the forward position just a few feet in front of me, my heart sank. I couldn't see past his helmeted head and shoulders. In the year since we'd last canoed, my son had grown half a foot taller. He might've been scrawny for a thirteen-year-old, but he was already too big for this boat.

We pushed off the bank and drifted with the current. I found that if I paddled the canoe at a slight angle, I could see downstream. This would work as long as we were on flat water, but I would have to straighten it out once we got to the rapids.

We paddled in loose formation, five boats spread out across the river. When War Woman appeared on the horizon, we fell into line, Michael out front in his duckie with me and Jackson close behind. Right off, I noticed a funnel-shaped wave blocking the chute down the top ledge. Michael blithely took the wave head on and flipped upside down. He bobbed to the surface, wide-eyed and sputtering, and kicked back into his duckie.

"We need to stay the hell away from the middle of that wave," I said to Jackson. "There's less curl closer to the rock."

"I see it."

Jackson drew the bow to the right. As we slipped past the wave, the stern jerked sideways beneath me. I flushed with that panic that overtakes you when you aren't sure how long the river will hold you in its grip, but this was just an admonition. The Chattooga let go, and we dropped safely down the ledge.

Roger followed our line and came through upright, but his deep-set eyes were caves of worry. More and more, as we tackled tougher rivers like the Pigeon and the Nolichucky, Roger's smile was giving way to a gape, as if the next rapid might do him in. Keith and I shared the concern that his skills were falling behind the rest of the group's, that it was only a matter of time before he got into trouble.

Roger insisted he would "get out and practice" between trips, but it was clear from the cobwebs in his canoe that he had not taken it out of the garage.

Beyond War Woman, the Chattooga picked up speed. Nameless rapids grew into daunting wave trains. We dodged left and right, trying to avoid the bigger waves, but water poured over the gunwales and sloshed around the hull.

Jackson moaned, "My feet are soaked."

"Wiggle your toes," I told him. "Keep 'em warm."

I spotted a familiar rock formation on river left and realized we were in the middle of Rock Garden. Normally, the current slowed through this stretch, but today, it pulled us along at a runner's speed. I attempted to interest Jackson in the curious rock slabs, but his focus was paralyzed by the tumbling river ahead.

We drifted beneath a cantilevered boulder to the head of a roaring rapid. The boat angled downward and started to buck. I leaned out to see ahead. Suddenly, we were upside down. I struggled to the surface and caught my bearings, icy waves breaking in my face. Jackson was just ahead of me, the upturned hull of the canoe to one side.

"Keep your feet up!" I yelled.

We bobbed through the waves — three, four, five, six.

"Head for shore!"

I rolled onto my side and started kicking, paddle in one hand, stern line in the other. Yards from shore, I lowered my feet and tried to stand. The canoe swung at the end of the rope and pulled me off balance. I fell face first into the water, windmilled my free arm toward the bank, grabbed a root and held on.

Randy appeared in his kayak and drove the canoe onto a sandbar. Jackson crawled out and stood shivering on the bank. I scrambled along the bank and grabbed the water-filled boat.

"Help me with this," I said to Jackson.

"I can't, Dad. I'm freezing."

"Then just stand there doing nothing," I said. "That's bound to warm you up."

My sarcasm worked no better on Jackson than my father's had with me. Jackson stomped his feet, scrunched his eyes.

Keith arrived and helped me flip the canoe.

"I can't see a damn thing in this boat!" I said. "Jackson's gotten too big."

Keith nodded. "It's tough."

With the boat secured, I turned back to Jackson. He had yet to move from his spot on the sandbar, possessed now by the cold. I walked over and put my arm around him, rubbed his shoulder hard.

"This wasn't your fault," I said. "You were doing fine."

"So what happened?" he asked.

"I don't know. I leaned out to try to see the rapid."

"Don't do that again."

Making up was hard for me. I was more inclined to harbor a grudge while Jackson was straightforward with his emotions. He could be petulant, for sure, and was prone to pass on the blame for his mistakes. But he didn't hesitate to put a hand on your back if he thought you were in pain.

We settled back into the canoe, knees pressed against the damp hull. The air temperature couldn't have been much above sixty, the sky fractured in gray and blue. So much for the weatherman's prediction of a warm, sunny day.

Despite my assurances to Jackson that everything would be all right, I knew we could not run these rapids blind. An experienced bowman could call out the route, but my son wasn't ready for that. In fact, he might never be ready for that. It dawned on me then that Jackson was really here to please me, that he would much rather be at home playing a video game. What had I gotten him into?

We dropped back to the middle of the pack and managed the next few bends without incident. In the distance, jets of spray danced above the water line — Dick's Creek Ledge.

The big humpbacked rock we normally landed on to scout the rapid lay all but submerged. We gathered in a tight cluster and stared at the thundering river.

"Are you sure this is Dick's Creek Ledge?" Michael said.

The high water had turned the distinctive route down the double drop on river left into a maelstrom of indecipherable cross-currents. The pillowed rock threw up a geyser six feet high. The ledge to river right, normally dry enough to walk across, was now a roaring spillway.

Keith had lately adopted the practice on our canoe trips of sucking on an unlit cigar. Reaching into the front pocket of his life vest, he pulled one out of a zip-lock bag and stuck it in the side of his mouth, distorting his cheek.

"Looks like the right-hand side is the only way," he said.

Charlie frowned. "I don't know. The bottom looks pretty squirrelly."

While the rest of us conferred, Randy jumped into his kayak and paddled straight down the left-hand chute. He launched off the pillowed rock, soared a dozen feet through the air, and landed upright at the bottom of the ledge.

Roger shook his head. "Randy's got balls."

Charlie smiled. "That's my brother."

The longer I looked at this rapid, the more frightened I became. I told Jackson he needed to portage this one. We paddled to the near shore, where I left him on the bank.

As I paddled past the scouting rock, Charlie called after me. "Which route are you going to take?"

I pointed at the six-foot-high ledge where the river spilled over in an even sheet.

"Where exactly?"

I shook my head. Sometimes in river running you just have to commit, pick a general route and hope for the best. You can't know how every boil, every cross-current will affect your canoe. You read the river as it unfolds.

I reached the still water above the ledge and rose up on my knees. The sheer drop hid the landing zone, but I conjured the image of what appeared to be the safest route. I paddled to the edge and held my breath. The bow pitched downward. Blood rushed to my head. I landed upright with a slap to the butt, like doing a cannonball off the diving board. The canoe glided to a halt. I turned to my friends and shrugged. "Piece of cake," I hollered.

How is it, I wondered, that obstacles that appear so daunting often turn out to be easy, while the unnamed threats do us in? That's the way it often is with rivers. Many a great paddler—men and women who have survived the most horrendous drops—have lost their lives on a simple Class III rapid. It could be that they weren't paying attention. Perhaps the odds of dying are simply higher given the sheer number of Class IIIs people run. Or perhaps, as the fatalists say, it was just their time.

I waved my paddle in the air, signaling the others to follow my route. Everyone landed upright, surprised as I was at his good fortune. Even Jackson sounded upbeat when I reached him onshore.

"I could have run that, Dad," he said.

"We'll do it together next time."

Beyond Dick's Creek, the hills closed in and the gradient of the river increased. Rapids came back to back, their steady roar drowning out our shouted commands. The river forked around a wooded island. Three boat lengths ahead of us, Charlie dropped into a hole and emerged full of water. I angled the canoe, looking for a smoother descent over the ledge. Jackson called out in alarm. "Dad, what are you doing?"

The turbulent water ran bank to bank. I hurried to straighten the canoe, but it was too late. We hit the hole at an angle and started to roll. *This can't happen again. I won't let it happen.* I threw my weight in the opposite direction, trying to counter the current's force. For an instant, we hung in a perilous balance. Then the canoe capsized.

When I surfaced this time, we were being carried at a dead sprint. A fallen tree lay halfway across the channel. I yelled at Jackson to get away. He started to swim, grazed the jagged end, and spun free. Just as I slipped past, the canoe slammed into the trunk and pinned.

Another rapid loomed ahead. I swam for the island and clawed my way onto shore. Randy flew past in his kayak, chasing after Jackson. My son was yards away from the next drop when Randy caught up with him.

"Grab on!" Randy yelled, swinging the stern of his kayak around.

With Jackson clinging to a loop of rope, Randy paddled hard for the island. He drove the kayak into the shallows. Jackson let go, stood in the knee-deep water, and tried to walk, but his elastic pants ballooned with water and weighted his feet to the bottom.

Keith and Charlie ran their boats ashore.

"I've got Jackson," Charlie said. "Help John with the boat."

Charlie helped Jackson ashore. My son was unhurt but thoroughly shaken. He stood with his arms straight, water pouring from his sleeves.

Keith and I scrambled back up the bank until we got to my canoe. I was relieved to see that it was pinned against the tree with the open hull facing downstream. Bow line and stern line fishtailed in the current. If we could reach one of those, we might be able to pull the boat loose.

I examined the old loblolly pine, its barrel-thick trunk slanted down at a forty-five-degree angle into the raging river. If someone could rig a rope for me to hold onto, I could crawl down to the boat.

Keith sounded skeptical. "You sure you want to do that?"

"I can get down all right, but I might need help getting up."

Randy arrived with a length of rope and lashed it to the broken stump. I wrapped one arm around the rope and the other around the rough bark. Crawling backward, I eased down the trunk until my feet touched the canoe. I kicked the hull, but the current held it tight. I lowered myself farther and kicked again.

"Fucker's pinned tight," I said.

Keith pointed at the rope trailing out from the stern. "Can you get ahold of that?"

I glanced down. There was no way to reach it with my hand, but I might snag it with my foot. I dangled my neoprene bootie in the current and hooked the underside of the rope. Twice it fell off. The third time, it stayed.

"Give me some tension!" I yelled.

Keith pulled on the safety rope, and I inched upward like a caterpillar. An arm's length from the bank, I handed the stern line to Randy. He gave it a hard yank, and the canoe swung free.

I rolled off the tree and brushed the bark from my paddle jacket. Keith and Charlie blocked my path.

"You and Jackson need to get off the river," Keith said. "Sandy Ford is just around the bend. You can pull out there and hike up the trail."

I stared back. No one had ever told me to get off a river.

"You don't want this to be the last time Jackson ever canoes," Charlie said. "If you flip again, that could do it."

Jackson huddled on the shore, his lips a bloodless purple, his arms around his shoulders. They were right. I had no business even thinking of going on.

"How do we get back to camp?" I asked.

Keith shrugged. "You can hitch a ride when you get to the road. If not, it's only a couple miles back to the put-in. I'll give you the keys to the van."

I relayed the news to Jackson, explaining there was a take-out just around the bend.

"I'm not getting back in that canoe," he said.

"We're on an island," I said. "We have to paddle off."

I promised we would not tip over again, but there was no bargaining with the Chattooga. We launched into the river and entered another maze of whitewater. We hit a rock, spun three-hundred-sixty degrees. Jackson grabbed the gunwales.

"Get me off!" he wailed. "Just get me off!"

Finally, the rapids subsided. A sandbar emerged on river left. I drove the canoe ashore and held it fast. Jackson stepped out and wiped the tears from his eyes.

"We made it, buddy," I said.

The rest of the crew pulled in beside us. I rolled the canoe over and drained it out. Keith held out the keys to the van.

"I guess we'll see you this afternoon," he said.

The sight of my friends still in their boats, ready to head off without me, was almost more than I could bear. I thanked them for their help and wished them a half-hearted good luck. Roger stepped out of his canoe.

"I've had enough of the Chattooga for today," he said. "I think I'll hike out with John and Jackson."

"You don't have to do that," I said.

Roger smiled. "No, it's fine."

I wanted to hug him. Roger might have been worried about his own safety, but he was doing this for me and, especially, for Jackson. Out of all the people here, including me, Roger alone knew what my son was feeling.

As our friends headed off, Jackson gave them a wave. "Thanks for helping me, Randy," he said. "You saved my life."

Roger and I slung our bow lines across our shoulders and started up the path with our canoes. Jackson trod ahead carrying a brace of paddles. I thought of what had almost happened to him on the river. A couple of inches to the left and he would have been pinned between the tree and the canoe. That would have been the end of it.

My mouth filled with the taste of metal filings, a sensation I'd experienced only twice before. The first time was when the firemen pulled Carrie McCune from the millstream. The other was on the Chagrin.

During Christmas vacation of my freshmen year at Yale, a warm front passed through northern Ohio. The ice thawed on the Chagrin and a group of us foolishly decided to run it. Dad and my brother paddled the Folbot, Rusty and I the little Grumman, and my friends Peter and Pat their own canoe. Halfway to Johnny Cake Ridge Road, a monster wave swamped both canoes. Rusty and I swam to shore as the Grumman sank beneath us. Peter rode his boat around the bend to safety, but Pat remained caught in a midstream eddy. He dog-paddled in circles in the frigid water, quickly losing strength. My mouth went dry. I could see death's gray hand rise from the river. Then Dad and my brother swooped down in the Folbot and hauled Pat to shore. The caustic taste dissolved to the sweetness of a son's pride in his father and the gift of life restored.

Roger, Jackson, and I reached the top of the gorge just as the sun broke through the clouds. Steam rose off our clothes as we walked down the dirt road. We made it back to the van in less than an hour.

That night our campsite resounded with familiar laughter. My friends had completed a successful run down the Chattooga at the highest water level we had ever faced. Jackson, too, was feeling good, unabashedly recounting the details of our calamity, burning marshmallows the way he liked them. I took a sip of Jack Daniels and passed it to Keith. I was still trying to make sense of what had happened on the river and where to go from here. Jackson was no longer a child whom I could blithely steer through the rapids. He would no longer assume that I could protect him from all harm. Maybe it was best that I paddle solo. There were more river dragons yet to slay, and rather than risk my son, I should face them on my own.

CHAPTER THIRTEEN

The Ocoee

After our scare on the Chattooga, Jackson and I made a handful of runs down the Haw, though he never enjoyed it. He'd seen all he wanted of whitewater. He became passionate about music and put down the paddle for a Fender guitar.

I was hurt that Jackson didn't share my love of canoeing, but I knew better than to try to push him. That would have been as fruitless as my father's attempts to get me to join the Cleveland corporate world. In recent years, I had even grown dissatisfied with my own choice to work for a non-profit. The public no longer seemed interested in saving energy and our projects began to flounder for lack of a committed audience.

Nights, I lay awake dreaming of writing while Cathy dozed beside me. When a job came open at a news magazine in Research Triangle Park, I applied and was accepted. I immersed myself in the assignments, happier than I'd been in years.

My father was dismayed, of course. Why would I take a 30 percent pay cut to write for a no-name magazine? How was I going to afford proper schooling for Jackson and Allison, summer camps and vacations abroad?

As we sat on the terrace in Gates Mills, I presented Dad with the magazine featuring a cover story I'd written on canoeing. He refused to take it from me. I set the magazine on the table hoping he would pick it up after I went back inside. But when I came out the next morning, it remained in the same spot, unmoved.

Dad was sick with cancer then and had less than a year to live. What little influence he'd exerted on his children's careers was about to disappear. We were going down paths he could not understand—Susie, a media relations officer for the United Nations; Peter an ethnomusicology professor; Annie an analyst for Human Rights Watch. And now I had turned to writing. My mother insisted that Dad was proud of us all, but he seemed loathe to express it.

I knew that I held my own grudge against my father, which affected me more than I liked to admit. Cathy had seen it through the years in my outbursts of sarcasm, in the bad dreams that pulled me awake and left me sweating at the edge of the bed. But I found no point in bringing it up at this stage in my life—in the prescience of my father's death. I had a loving relationship with my wife and children. I was pursuing the career I wanted. That should have been enough.

Keith and I floated in the eddy below Nantahala Falls. He'd already surfed the steep wave at the bottom once, having ferried upstream until he hung suspended atop the curling hand that magically held the canoe in place. Now it was my turn.

The bottom of the rapid was maybe thirty feet away, nothing that a competent canoeist couldn't reach. I paddled upstream and started to work my way across the current. As I neared the wave, my stroke faltered. What if the water grabbed me and wouldn't let go? What if it drew me in? The current swatted the nose around and sent my canoe spinning downstream. I hurried back to the shelter of the eddy.

Keith shook his head and rolled his cigar to the side of his mouth. "You suck at ferrying," he said.

Twice more I approached the wave and each time I backed off. "Fuck it," I said. I didn't need to learn how to ferry to get down the Nantahala or any of the other rivers we canoed. But Keith's jab bothered me. How could I call myself a canoeist if I didn't know how to ferry?

And there was more. Every now and then, Keith brought up my less admirable behavior from our work years ago at the Alternative Energy Corporation—my tendency to bail out of difficult tasks, to trash my boss behind his back as I had done with my father. Sarcasm and subterfuge were my weapons for dealing with resentment.

I stared at the tumbling water. My tenure at the AEC lay ten years in the past and my father had been dead nearly that long. I either needed to accept my limitations or do something about them.

Two weeks later, I called the Nantahala Outdoor Center and asked for a private lesson. "I want to take it on the Ocoee," I said, enunciating that hard "c." "I might be bringing a friend."

The Ocoee. The big one. Years before, Keith had run this legendary Tennessee mountain river and come back raving about monster waves and savage cross-currents. Though he managed to come through unscathed, he confessed to being terrified the whole way down. He also allowed he'd be willing to run it again some day.

Keith hesitated when I called. "I was afraid you were going to ask," he said. "Let me talk to Karen."

I was willing to take the lesson alone, but having Keith along, even if he was paddling his own canoe, would boost my courage. And however it turned out, I wanted Keith to know that I'd tried.

"All right, damn it, I'll come." he said.

Keith and I headed to the Nantahala on a Friday afternoon. We were to meet our instructor in the morning and drive over the Snowbird Mountains to the Ocoee. After setting up camp, we visited the Outdoor Center to check out the latest equipment. It was all kayak stuff now, squat little boats that resembled wooden clogs, designed strictly for playing in the rapids. The notion of running a river from beginning to end was passé. People were in it just for the thrills.

I picked up a guidebook on the Ocoee and brought it to the counter.

"Gonna kayak the bad boy?" the clerk said.

"Nope. Canoe."

He raised his eyebrows. "Good luck."

The guidebook described each rapid on the river, ending with a section called "Screw-up factor," which forewarned what might happen if you botched the run. "Double Suck" earned a screw-up factor of nine out of ten. *"The rock that creates it is not far below the surface, and can do cervical damage to the unsuspecting hole surfer,"* the book said. *"If you end up in there, tuck tight in case of a flip. And do try to take a deep breath before you flip, because you may be in there for awhile."*

Years before, a woman giving me a haircut had told me how her husband had fallen out of a raft on a whitewater river and gotten caught in a hole like Double Suck. While the others watched helplessly, he spun around sideways, unable to escape. He drowned within minutes, but even then, the river would not give him up. In order to dislodge his body, a rescue team was forced to cut down a tree and float it through the rapid. Lying in my tent the night before my lesson, I became that man, forever in the river, forever drowning.

A dog barked in the pre-dawn darkness. I crawled out of my sleeping bag and headed for the wash house nursing a bad case of the runs. The toilet seat was cold, the air foul. I thought of Cathy, Jackson, and Allison at home and warm in their beds. Thank God, I hadn't dragged Jackson in on this.

At first light, Keith and I drove down to River's End Restaurant and ordered breakfast. I couldn't eat.

"Are you sure you're ready for this?" Keith asked.

I nodded without conviction.

"You need to eat something."

We paid our bill and stopped in a convenience store down the road. I bought a couple of bananas, hoping I could keep these down. After another trip to the bathroom, I donned my river clothes.

Bob Beasley looked to be in his mid-forties, with wire-rimmed glasses and a receding hairline. He welcomed us into the office at the NOC complex and had us sign some release forms.

"So what have you guys done before?" he asked.

I blurted out the names — Chattooga, Pigeon, French Broad, Nolichucky. I nodded at Keith. "He's done the Ocoee. I haven't."

Bob smiled. "You'll be fine."

We loaded Bob's mango-colored canoe onto our trailer and drove west into Tennessee. Keith's way of relieving tension was to talk, and his enthusiastic recounting of our exploits on the rivers buoyed my spirits. Just past Ducktown, the road angles downhill, descending into the Ocoee watershed. My stomach began to tighten.

Like the Nantahala and the Pigeon, the Ocoee is a dam-controlled river, and on days when water is being released, boaters converge from all over the Southeast. The parking lot at the put-in teemed with whitewater diehards and novices alike. Rafters milled like cattle around the buses. Kayakers pulled paddles and wetsuits from the raised tailgates of SUVs. I was eager to get on the river, but Bob had other plans.

To one side of the parking lot lay a lake created by Ocoee Dam Number 2. Bob announced we were going to perform an hour of warm-up exercises on flat water before we hit the river. *Bullshit. I came to paddle whitewater.*

"I want you guys to paddle about thirty yards out, turn around and come back," Bob said. "I want you to keep a straight line."

Paddle a straight line? That should be easy enough. Using my best J-stroke, I set off across the lake.

"Try using a pry, John," Bob said.

I glanced over my shoulder. "What's wrong with the J-stroke?"

"That's fine for flat water, but it's too slow for Class IV rapids. You need short strokes that will instantly adjust your direction."

I shook my head. At Keewaydin, we had laughed at the kids who used a jerky pry at the end of their stroke instead of the more graceful J. It was a sign of poor instruction or none at all.

"Turn around and come back paddling on the other side," Bob said.

I switched hands. Bob frowned. "You need to learn to paddle on both sides without changing grips."

I said I'd never been told you couldn't switch grips. Bob shook his head. "The half-second it takes you to change hands is a half-second you may need to get out of trouble. And every time you let go of the paddle, you run the risk of dropping it. You can't do that on the Ocoee."

I tried paddling on the "off side" with my forearm extended across my stomach. I could bring the paddle backward but couldn't lift it clear of the water on my retrieve. Bob climbed in his canoe and came out to help me. Placing his hands atop mine, he demonstrated how to execute the stroke.

"Turn the blade sideways at the end of your stroke and bring it forward through the water," he said.

I felt embarrassed to have the instructor put his hands on mine. I struggled with the stroke a few more times, then gave up.

"Keep trying," Bob said. "You'll get it."

Meanwhile, Keith, who'd learned canoeing from God knows where, was earning nothing but praise. I'd seen him use these strokes on the river but thought he was showboating.

At noon, Bob called the practice to a halt. We pulled our boats ashore and ate lunch beside the lake. The parking lot was quiet; the rafters gone downriver. So much for getting ahead of the crowd.

"What are you thinking, John?" Bob asked.

I confessed to being scared, that I was counting on him to get me safely down the river.

"I'll show you the way to go, but you're going to have to get there yourself," he said.

I nodded grimly. "Let's do it."

❧

The put-in at the Ocoee can intimidate even the best paddlers. Water thunders over a thirty-foot-high dam and surges through an impassable boulder field on the near side of the river. The open channel lies a hundred yards out, requiring paddlers to make their way across the current without losing ground.

Bob knew about my poor ferrying skills and offered to show me a "cheat route" along the near shore. My goal for the day had been to learn the things I'd shied away from, but now I followed him through the boulders like an obedient child.

We gathered in the eddy of House Rock, whose bulk offered us shelter from the raging current. Below us loomed Grumpy Ledge, an indecipherable maze of shallows and holes. This time, there was no cheat route. Bob gave us the basic instructions for ferrying to the far side of the river.

"Come out of the eddy at a ten-degree angle," he said. "Take short strokes and use a pry to make any corrections. John, you follow after me."

Moving with seemingly effortless strokes, Bob ferried across the river until he reached the open channel.

"Go get 'em," Keith said.

I paddled out from behind the rock and started to work my way to the far side. The current rushed beneath the hull. I countered with urgent strokes. Halfway across, I started to panic. I wasn't making progress. My arms began to tire. Desperate to reach the open channel, I increased the angle of my ferry, and the current pushed the nose downstream toward Grumpy Ledge. I raced back to House Rock.

"Don't say anything," I said to Keith. "I can do it."

There comes a time when you grow tired of repeating the same mistakes. Something clicks in your mind, and you know it's time for a change. When I paddled out from behind House Rock the second time, I held my line. I worked the boat across the river, keeping the bow at a narrow angle to the current. When I reached the open channel, I turned and bounced through the waves. Bob was waiting in the eddy.

"Better," he said.

I surveyed the river ahead. Steep hills rose to both sides. Traffic whined along the narrow highway to the south; a giant wooden flume carrying water to a downstream powerhouse loomed to the north. The Ocoee would never be called a scenic river, but it had no shortage of rapids.

All across the channel, kayakers darted between boulders and surfed the countless waves and chutes. The rafts clustered in the middle, lining up to run the main rapids. I had imagined the big, slow rafts would provide me some reassurance, but they were like herds of elephants, blocking the view, knocking smaller boats aside.

"Ten points for every canoe we flatten," I heard one of the guides say.

Deftly moving among the rafts and boulders, Bob led us through

Gonzo Shoals and Broken Nose. We "boofed" Double Suck, avoiding the treacherous hole by jerking sideways over a smooth, dry ledge and landing with a hollow thud in the calm water below.

I began to feel confident that we could avoid the worst rapids. Then, the Ocoee narrowed and dropped into an enormous wave train.

"Best way to run this is to hug the right side and duck out of the waves as soon as possible," Bob said of Double Trouble. "If you get stuck in the middle, keep paddling."

I stared at the tongue of water disappearing over the edge downstream of us. The drop had to be at least six feet and the waves beyond just as high. The road lay just up the bank. I could easily opt out of running this rapid. And I would learn nothing.

I took a few strokes to get clear of the rocks. The full rapid came into view, and I realized I was being swept toward the middle. My stomach rushed to my head as the canoe slid down and up the first wave.

"Paddle!" Bob called behind me.

I used the pry and tried to straighten the canoe. I flew up the second wave and slid down at an angle.

"Keep paddling!"

The canoe rose a third time and teetered on the crest. I couldn't hold my line. I was rolling under.

⮟

On my father's last evening, August sunlight streamed through the bay window into my parents' bedroom. The drug capsules glowed orange on the nightstand, useless now that Dad could no longer swallow.

Mom came into the room and ran a hand over his forehead. Dad could not open his eyes. His breathing had become suddenly labored.

"I don't think he's going to make it through the night," she said.

I felt a moment of panic. "Are you serious?"

"I'd better call the doctor."

Prior to my last visit, I had written Dad a letter. I expressed my sorrow that he could no longer drink his favorite wine, entertain guests, or even walk to the sun porch to look over his beloved Chagrin. I acknowledged that he had lost many things but said he had not lost his children. "I know that you loved us," I managed to write.

Dad never read my magazine, but when I next came back to Gates Mills, he held up the letter.

"Thank you for this," he said and did not look away.

I met his gaze and offered a tight-lipped, "You're welcome." We could say more at another time, I thought.

Mom left the room to call the doctor, and I was alone again with Dad. My heart was pounding, my breathing rapid. I needed it to be like this, for him not to be able to respond. I got up from my chair, crossed the room, and sat on the bed. I took his hand and began to talk.

I thanked my father for everything he'd given me—the good schools, the summer camps, the canoe. I confessed he'd been right about the important things in life. He had seen the beauty in nature and honored it in his way. He had married my mother and stayed true to her to the end. He enjoyed good friends. He provided for his children. I didn't say I loved him. There were too many other emotions in the way. But I could feel it pooling like water behind a ledge.

JOHN MANUEL ❧ 207

My mother arrived with the doctor close behind. I squeezed Dad's hand and let go.

⊸⊷

I remember rolling under the canoe, the way the water muffled the roar of the rapid and softened the sun's glare. All around me were bubbles, millions and millions of them, rushing along at the same speed. *We are like this—souls traveling through space. We are born in the tumult of the river, carried along by forces we cannot control. And we're also beautiful in the way we hold the light, murmuring to one another on this journey toward the surface, our short, spiraling lives.*

I stayed under for a long time, safe from the waves crashing overhead. The water ran warm and deep. There was no need to panic, but my air was running out. I kicked out of the thigh straps and burst into daylight.

Bob's canoe appeared beside me.

"You all right?" he asked.

"Yeah. Water's fine."

"You got stuck in the middle."

"Happens a lot," I said.

Bob smiled and headed off after my boat. Keith arrived and told me to grab onto his stern.

"Christ, I thought you were a goner. You disappeared after the third wave."

I passed it off. "It was cool, man."

We paddled down to where Bob held my boat. I hauled the Caption onto the rocks and drained out the water. Bob suggested we take a break.

I stripped off my life vest and shirt and laid them out to dry. Keith dropped down beside me and held out a juice box. I stared back the way we had come. Sunlight sparkled atop the waves I'd just swum through. It wasn't so bad getting dunked. I felt baptized, washed of the sin of pride.

"So, what do you think about the Ocoee?" Keith asked.

"It's great," I said.

"Serious?"

"Yeah, man. This is just what I need."

Keith smiled and slapped my back.

Shouts rose above the rush of water. A trio of kayakers bobbed through Double Trouble. They circled in an eddy like water bugs and took turns darting in and out of the waves. When they'd had their fill of enders and three-sixties, they turned and drifted along the near shore.

"Bob, is that you?" a woman called.

She spoke with an Australian accent, flashed a gorgeous smile and sea-blue eyes. "What are you doing here, man?"

Bob explained he was giving Keith and me a canoeing lesson.

"Canoeing, eh? I'm quite impressed." Turning to me, she asked, "Has there been much carnage?"

I laughed at her pronunciation. *Kahnidge.* That had to be lingo among the veteran river runners. I thought about my humiliation at the lake, my botched ferry at Grumpy Ledge, my capsize on Double Trouble. In retrospect, they didn't amount to much.

"No, not much carnage," I said.

"Well, carry on. One big daddy left."

She headed off downstream, double blade flashing in the sun.

"So what's the big daddy?" I asked Bob.

"Tablesaw," he said. "It's basically an enormous wave train. It looks pretty intimidating, but it won't kill you."

"Are you sure?"

Bob smiled. "I haven't lost anyone yet."

I paddled the next mile dizzy with visions of jagged, white-tipped waves whirring in front of me. I replayed in my mind what had gone wrong on Double Trouble. This time I would hold my line no matter what.

A herd of rafts gathered at the head of a rocky narrows. One by one, they disappeared from view, the passengers' screams muffled as they fell. My stomach tightened again. We reached the top of Tablesaw and huddled by the shore.

Bob yelled above the thundering rapid. "Best way to take this one is right down the middle. You'll need to ferry out to get in position… John?"

Before this day, no one could have convinced me that such a rapid could be run in a canoe. The craft was not made for waves like this, taller than a man, running for dozens of yards. If you got off line you were sure to capsize. But if I could keep the boat straight, I might have a chance.

"Right down the middle?" I asked.

"Just follow the V," Bob said. His advice echoed the instructions my father had given me for that first rapid on the Chagrin.

I crept to the edge. A twenty-yard ferry would put me in good position. Anything less would be disaster. I aimed upstream and paddled into the current. Water raced beneath the hull pushing me back. *Easy, now. Don't panic.* I worked my way into mid-channel. Another stroke for good measure. *Now, turn and lean…*

I shot down the entry and up the face of the first wave. Paddle, pry, paddle, pry. A second wave rose, and then a third. Paddle, pry, paddle pry. I blew the spray from my mouth, kept the bow running straight. Paddle, pry, paddle pry.

Then the waves began to subside. The canoe stopped bucking. Keith caught up to me, smiling.

"We did it, man," he said.

"That's it?" I kept my paddle in the water, wary of the still powerful current.

"Yes! We're through."

A stream of foam played out before me, a long white beard tapering to rippling jade. We slid into the pool, one behind the other, carving perfect half-circles as we turned into the eddy. The bubbles crackled as they burst into daylight. I shipped my paddle and drifted.

The Cuyahoga

In December, 1974, Congress passed Public Law 93-555, creating the Cuyahoga Valley National Recreation Area. The recreation area was designated as the Cuyahoga Valley National Park in 2000. The park encompasses 33,000 acres and draws more than three million visitors a year, making it the seventh most visited national park in the country. The main attractions are the Ohio & Erie Canal Towpath (now used as a bike path) and the Cuyahoga Valley Scenic Railroad, both of which parallel the Cuyahoga River.

The Cuyahoga River through the park remains polluted, though not nearly as bad as it was in the 1970s. The river looks and smells normal for much of the year and even supports springtime runs of steelhead trout. During periods of heavy rain, Akron's Combined Sewer Outflow still poses a threat to the river. The city's long-term plans call for upgrading the sewage treatment facilities to be able to handle peak flows. Until that happens, the Park Service does not recommend canoeing or kayaking the river.

The Pigeon

The Pigeon River in Tennessee has become one of the most popular whitewater rafting runs in the Southeast. Half-a-dozen outfitters carry more than a hundred thousand customers down the river each year, adding hundreds of thousands of dollars to the Cocke County tax revenues. Jerry Taylor's Smokey Mountain River Company was taken over by his daughter following his death, but has since shut down.

In 1999, Champion International sold the pulp and paper mill in Canton to its workers, who formed Blue Ridge Paper Products, Inc. The mill continues to make improvements to its production processes, though nothing as dramatic as its major modernization during the 1990s. Water quality in the Pigeon is much better than it was prior to the upgrade. Water color is still an issue, especially during periods of drought, when the relatively high volume of effluent from the mill turns the river noticeably darker.

The plant's North Carolina wastewater discharge permit comes up for renewal every five years. In hopes of forcing stricter color requirements, groups such as Clean Water for North Carolina and the

American Canoe Association have requested that the Environmental Protection Agency intervene in the permit renewal process. The EPA has so far declined to do so.